400

The Art of Simple French Cookery

The Art of
Simple French Cookery

ALEXANDER WATT

DOUBLEDAY & COMPANY, INC.

GARDEN CITY, NEW YORK

Library of Congress Catalog Card Number 62-11290

Contents

Recipes for asterisked items [*] may be found by consulting the index.

Foreword

This cookbook, on the art of simple French cooking, has been inspired by Alexandre Dumaine, the chef-proprietor of the renowned Hôtel de la Côte d'Or, at Saulieu, who made the remark one day when we were discussing the various aspects of *la cuisine française*, that "the simplest dishes are often the most difficult to prepare to perfection."

In *Paris Cuisine* (published in 1953), written in collaboration with James Beard, there appeared one hundred and sixty recipes, several of them requiring considerable skill and patience in the private kitchen.

In *Paris Bistro Cookery* (published in 1957), I aimed at giving one hundred simpler, more easily prepared dishes. Now, in *The Art of Simple French Cookery*, I have gone a stage further and give one hundred and twenty-eight even simpler recipes. All of them are new, or differ in some way from those given in the other two books. These are essentially easy dishes to cook; some may take more time to prepare than others, but none of them are complicated, neither do they require rare or expensive ingredients. Several may appear, at first sight, to be mere repeats of certain standard French recipes that are to be found in most cookbooks. But, if read carefully, it will be seen either that the cooking process has been modified, or that some ingredients have been added to, or substituted for others, in the recipes.

All of the eleven sauces that appear in this cookbook are easy to make. I have intentionally avoided those that require the use of *fonds de veau* (heavy veal stock), the recipe of which is given, in *Paris Cuisine* and in *Paris Bistro Cookery* for the preparation of more involved and richer sauces.

I have tried, throughout the book, to vary the nature of the dishes as much as possible, in order to cater for a cross-section of the public who, for specific reasons, may be interested in different methods and time limits of cooking. For example, there are dishes that are easily and rapidly prepared in a matter of minutes, such as the Foies de Volaille André.* Others, also easily prepared, take longer to cook, like the Boeuf Danois,* which you can safely leave to simmer for three hours while you do the household chores.

There are numerous very economical dishes, like the Beignets aux Pommes de Terre*; and I have included "labor-saving" dishes, such as the Curry à l'Indo-Chinoise* which, like several others in the book, *improve* on being reheated. For large families, there are soups and stews, like La Potée,* which serve eight, ten, twelve persons. Likewise, there are what I term "multipurpose" recipes, like the Pot-au-Feu à la Langue de Veau,* from which four separate dishes can be made.

Original and entertaining recipes appear, too, like the Figues au Jambon Fumé*; and unusual combinations, like Porc à l'Orange.* The use of herbs is strongly recommended for certain simple dishes as, for example, with the Grondin Rôti, Beurre Montpensier.* Finally, there are recipes that do not appear in any cookbook, such as Monsieur Quinson's amusing Irish Stew à la Provençale.*

Useful hints and suggestions for preparing and for improving the dishes, appear in the text (in italics) of several of the recipes. These may prove of assistance to less experienced cooks.

Apart from the fifty-six recipes that have been extracted from my own repertoire of dishes—I have had to omit several that appear elsewhere in the book in some form or other—that we prepare in our Paris kitchen, I have collected these recipes from widely different sources; from the greatest living French chef to the humble fishmonger, and other back-room cooks of the Latin Quarter in Paris.

The proprietors of some of our favorite bistros have kindly let us in on some of their secrets, and eight new ones, with their recipes, have been added to the list of our latest discoveries; their names and addresses should be appended to *Paris Bistro Cookery*. The most famous of the Paris restaurateurs have also come up to scratch and have divulged What They Eat When Alone.

It is hoped that this medley of recipes may be a source of inspiration to those who are keen to experiment, in their own kitchens, with simple and satisfying dishes to be enjoyed by the family, and by discerning guests who appreciate *la bonne et honnête cuisine française*.

Some of these dishes have been demonstrated, by the author, on television; and others described by him in newspapers and magazines. Acknowledgments are made, therefore, to the following for insertion in this cookbook of their recipes:

> B.B.C. Television Service, London.
> The *Daily Telegraph*, London.
> *House and Garden*, New York.
> *Vogue* magazine, London, Paris, and New York.
> *Réalités* magazine, London, Paris, and New York.
> *Woman's Day*, New York.
> *Gentlemen's Quarterly*, New York.
> *Cuisine et Vins de France*, Paris.

The Art of Simple French Cookery

Culinary Introduction

Here are a few general principles that should be followed in the creation of the dishes that are given in this book. I trust that experienced cooks will forgive me for mentioning what, for them, must appear to be obvious. Nevertheless, I feel that insistence on the artistry of a profession or a hobby, be it painting or cooking, can bear repetition if it is for the benefit of those who may feel that they have not yet mastered certain techniques.

Most of the recipes given here are timed according to the use of earthenware pots, and copper and enamel pans, as distinct from aluminum utensils. But it is not every home that is in possession of such ware. So, if it has to be aluminum, then use the heavier kind, so as to be able to cook these dishes *à la minute* (i.e. for the exact time given). If thin aluminum pans are employed, then care must be taken to adjust accordingly the prescribed cooking time; for the food in the thin aluminum pan will heat centrifugally and cook too rapidly, instead of heating gradually and retaining a steady, even, overall temperature. This is of major importance in cooking.

Careful timing in cooking contributes greatly to Alexandre Dumaine's insistence on precision in the kitchen. A kitchen alarm clock and a keen interest in preparing food are about all that are required—provided the ingredients are of the best quality—to be able to succeed in perfecting simple dishes. A good test is to be able to prepare the Fillets of John Dory* and the accompanying Sauce Hollandaise* so that they are ready to be served together the minute that both of them are just cooked and no more.

It really is worth the effort to spend the little extra money, time and trouble in buying and cooking just the required amount of top-quality food, instead of playing around with an unnecessary amount of the second-best. It should be borne in mind that the presentation of a carefully prepared dish is of considerable importance. For example, it can make a great deal of difference as to how my Indo-Chinese Curry* dish is arranged and set on the table. It can easily be made to look both attractive and appetizing. Lack of interest or imagination will result in the opposite, distressing, effect.

In a few of these recipes, I state that the sauce should be reduced, or cooked gently, until it thickens. Careful and closely watched reduction and blending of a sauce can make all the difference to a dish which, in itself, may have required exacting measurements and preparation. So, surely, as far as sauces are concerned, it is worth both time and trouble to stay in the kitchen and to cook the sauces cautiously without having to go off to attend to other household matters.

That little extra patience in the kitchen will also be rewarded if you wish to please your guests by preparing your own Sauce Tomate,* Sauce Mayonnaise,* Sauce Hollandaise* (according to the easy recipes given here) instead of buying tasteless, commercial "concentrated" substitutes.

Whenever possible, use *dry* white wine, *wine* vinegar, and *fresh, unsweetened* cream in cooking. And when I mention butter, I mean *pure* butter, and not a substitute. Brillat-Savarin, the celebrated author of *The Physiology of Taste,* claimed that one of the basic principles of cooking was the use, in the kitchen, of the finest quality table butter.

The use of herbs and seasoning is also of great importance in both simple and classic French cooking. Here I have deliberately avoided naming, or advising the use of bottled flavoring products for these recipes. Instead, I give the different proportions for various herbs to be employed in their preparation. The judicious use of herbs and seasoning can, and does, make such a difference to soups and stews.

Two conclusions can be drawn from Alexandre Dumaine's remark that "exactness in cooking is difficult to achieve." One is that the difficulty resides in achieving the exact required result, according to the precise indications in the recipe; the other, that you have to reckon with your own particular taste and that of the family, or of your guests. We are not all born with uniform palates: you may like garlic, others may not; some prefer lemon juice, instead of vinegar, in the salad dressing, etc. There must, therefore, remain a margin in the prescribed amount of herbs and seasoning to be used in the preparation of these dishes.

For those not versed in menu French, I have translated each dish into English; this also means that there is a double index for the recipes.

French Recipe Terms

Beurre Manié: Butter and flour kneaded together and gradually added to a sauce so as to thicken it.

Blanchir: To place in boiling water so as to whiten, purify and loosen skins, principally of meats.

Blanquette: A meat stew (generally veal) with an egg-and-cream sauce and garnished with mushrooms and small onions.

Bouquet Garni: A bouquet of herbs basically composed of bay leaves, thyme and parsley, used to season soups, stews, sauces, and other dishes, so as to impart an added aromatic flavor.

Court Bouillon: A mixture of water, herbs, vegetables and either wine or vinegar, used mainly for cooking fish.

Croquettes: Small fish cakes, or meat and/or vegetable rissoles.

Croutons: Small triangular or heart-shaped slices of bread fried in butter.

Farci: Stuffed.

à la Ficelle: Suspended by, or attached to a length of string.

Fines Herbes: Parsley, chives, chervil, and tarragon finely chopped and mixed in equal parts.

Flambé: Blazed.

Fumet: Concentrated fish stock.

en Gelée: Cold, jellied.

Gibelotte: Meat (generally rabbit) stewed in wine in a casserole.

au Gratin: Sprinkled with bread crumbs, dotted with butter (and cheese) and browned in the oven.

Julienne: Meat, vegetables, fruit cut into matchstick, or broader, strips.

Marinate: To immerse food, for a calculated length of time, in a preparation of spices, condiments, vegetables, herbs, wine, and/or some other liquid so as to enhance its flavor.

Mirepoix: A flavoring employed mostly in braising meat, which is usually composed of finely diced, or chopped, carrots, leeks, onions, celery, lean bacon, and bay leaf and thyme, cooked gently in oil or in butter.

en Papillote: Fish, or meat, wrapped in greaseproof paper and cooked in the oven.

Paupiette: Thin, rolled, stuffed, escalope slice of meat.

Roux: A mixture of flour and butter, or fat, blended together over a low heat and which serves as the basic thickening agent for most sauces.

Sauté: To fry lightly and quickly in a small amount of butter or fat, tossing and turning, during the cooking process, instead of allowing to sizzle.

Velouté: A thick cream soup.

Alexandre Dumaine
and the Soul of Cooking

In my opinion—and it is that of countless other gourmets—
Alexandre Dumaine, the celebrated proprietor of the Hôtel
de la Côte d'Or, at Saulieu, is the greatest chef in France
today.

In the course of my gastronomic peregrinations, I have made
the acquaintance of most of the well-known chefs in Paris
and throughout France. But none I know of are as impas-
sioned with their culinary pursuit as Dumaine. During the
numerous discussions we have had together, concerning both
simple and classic French cooking, he has reiterated, with a
solemnity that commands respect, that for him "there exists
no finer profession."

Aside from the unique experience of enjoying to the full
his fabulous wine and food, you do not have to wait to get to
know Dumaine well before realizing the significance of this
statement. Any gourmet is bound on first meeting Dumaine
to feel himself in the presence of a great expert whose whole
life is consecrated to the fine art of gastronomy. In speaking
of what he terms "a civilized art," Dumaine relates his many
and varied culinary experiences with an earnestness that never
fails to impress. Anyone who might doubt his sincerity has
only to question his charming and most hospitable wife,
Jeanne Dumaine, who attends to the administration and re-
ceives the clientèle at the Hôtel de la Côte d'Or (180 miles
south of Paris, on Route Nationale No. 6) with a kindness and
psychological understanding that go to make it a haven of
comfort for exacting epicures.

According to Madame Dumaine, Alexandre lives in a world of non-stop cuisine. When he is not working in the kitchen, then he is experimenting with his recipes. He never stops thinking of *la cuisine;* he even dreams of it and, if at night he cannot sleep, then he sits up and studies new and different ways of preparing his *spécialités de la maison.* He cannot even let up when he and Madame Dumaine go off together for an annual fortnight's respite, in order to give the staff a holiday. All the comfort and relaxation that the beautiful Riviera can offer mean less to him than the confines of his small kitchen in Saulieu, where he prepares masterpieces for knowledgeable gastronomes who come from near and far to relish them.

Dumaine's Livre d'Or is priceless for the signatures it contains. The names of the famous that figure in it are too many for me to list here. Other documents on display, in the entrance to the restaurant, that are the envy of many a visiting chef, are the endless diplomas and medals that Dumaine has won as culinary prizes. He probably tops the list as the most decorated of French chefs. Here again, I will not attempt to enumerate them beyond saying that his most recent award, which is considered to be one of the highest that a chef can receive, is his nomination as Member of Honor of the Club des Cent, the most select and distinguished of gastronomic clubs in France.

How did Dumaine attain this enviable position? The answer, quite simply, is fifty years of sheer hard work and a passionate devotion to his profession. Every single one of the great chefs I have talked with has given me a similar account of an extremely hard apprenticeship which meant rising at dawn, if not before, and being the last to be left in the kitchen to clean up.

Dumaine was born at Digoin, in the Soane-et-Loire Département, in 1895. He started to learn his profession at the age of twelve when he became an apprentice in the local pastry shop. From there, he moved into the kitchens of the Hôtel de la Poste, at Paray-le-Monial. Later, he studied under the famous Aletti, at the Hôtel Carlton, in Vichy; and in Paris, under Léopold Mourier, at the Café de Paris which, to the profound regret of many a gourmet, closed its doors in 1955.

Dumaine started his Livre d'Or during the first world war with the names of two very prominent figures who were to herald his eventual triumphal success. They were Clemenceau and General Franchet d'Espèrey, for whom he cooked an impromptu meal up on the front. After the war, Dumaine was nominated *chef de cuisine* in several of the leading hotels in spas throughout the country. Eventually he was given the important job as director of the chain of hotels of the Sahara, owned by the Compagnie Transatlantique. In 1931 he retired from this post and acquired the Hôtel de la Côte d'Or, in Saulieu.

What made Dumaine wish to become a chef in the first place? It was a natural inclination to work in the kitchen ever since the days when, as a youngster, he used to watch his mother at home cooking the plain and excellent regional dishes of Lower Burgundy. The family was poor, but Dumaine's mother always succeeded in producing delicious food based on the simplest of recipes. It was from her that he learned the art of preparing simple dishes with studious care. And that is the very theme of this cookbook. By referring to Dumaine at some length, I have wished to stress the fact that the greatest living French chef, whose repertoire of dishes of *la haute cuisine française* is phenomenal, advocates the art of cooking simple food with diligent application.

On the back of the very impressive wine list of the Hôtel de la Côte d'Or (there are over four hundred different wines in the cellar) you will find a printed notice which reads:

Dear Client,
    The quality of the products that we employ and all the

care that we take in their preparation will always assure you an agreeable and classic meal. Nevertheless, if you have given us sufficient warning, at least the day before, you can taste, on your arrival, according to the season and to your taste:

Un feuilleté de queues d'écrevisses, un pâté de brochet, une matelote d'anguille, une truite au Chambord, un bisque d'écrevisses, un crème Saint Hubert, un jambon du pays aux quatres purées, ou un mille-feuille de jambon fourré au foie-gras, un ris de veau Nantua, un boeuf à la cuillère, un aspic de crêtes et de rognons de coq, un pâté de canard ou de gibier, un lièvre à la royale, un porcelet rôti et farci de boudins blancs et noirs, une poularde des Ducs de Bourgogne, un coq en pâte, un dindonneau Louis XIV ou

L'OREILLER DE LA BELLE-AURORE

c'est-à-dire une des belles préparations de la grande cuisine française.

There is nothing in the traditions of *la haute cuisine française* that Dumaine does not know how to prepare to perfection. The Oreiller de la Belle-Aurore, a masterpiece of culinary achievement, is an excellent example. This most magnificent of all pâtés is named after Brillat-Savarin's mother, Claudine-Aurore Récamier. The Oreiller, so called because it is shaped like a pillow, contains pheasant, woodcock, hare, pork, veal, foie-gras, truffles, and chicken livers. This fabulous dish is not one that can be prepared in a private kitchen. As Dumaine rightly says, one should not attempt to copy at home what the restaurateurs only can succeed in cooking in their own kitchens. "It is much better," says Dumaine, "that the housewife contents herself in perfecting unpretentious dishes. And that in itself is not always easy."

One of Dumaine's closest friends was Fernand Point, whose death in 1954 was a great loss to epicures throughout the world. Point was universally acclaimed as the greatest res-

taurateur in France, and certainly no connoisseur of wine
and food who was fortunate enough to know Point during his
lifetime and to have sampled his superb cuisine will disclaim
this. Dumaine and his fellow chefs held Point in the highest esteem: they affectionately and respectfully called him
"L'Empereur."

Point and Dumaine were two great artists who had much in
common. They both agreed absolutely on precision and perfection in cooking. "We don't invent," Dumaine once told me,
when speaking of Point who was then still alive, "we aim to
perfect. At the same time, you must admit that nothing is ever
perfect."

Herein lies the secret of the success of these two master
chefs. Like all great artists, they were never satisfied with
their efforts. Dumaine once declared that he had been making a certain not very complicated sauce for over thirty years
and it was only now that he thought he had succeeded in
getting the "right balance."

When we last called on Monsieur and Madame Dumaine,
we were invited to partake of a "simple" lunch. By general
standards this was far from simple fare, yet the main dish, a
Poularde au Vapeur du Pot-au-Feu, in its actual preparation,
was certainly not complicated and can be prepared by any
cook who has the time and the patience to do so. As I myself
have discovered to my own benefit, time and patience in the
kitchen are the forerunners of the precision and perfection
that Dumaine states to be the ultimate attainment of French
cuisine.

"In its own way, there is no more perfect dish than my
Poularde au Vapeur, the discovery of a magistrate of Bugey
and a compatriot of the great Brillat-Savarin," said Dumaine.
"It should be cooked in a large earthenware pot of twelve
quarts capacity. You start by preparing a Pot-au-Feu* with
beef, ox-tail, chicken giblets, and all the usual vegetables and

herbs. After this has simmered for four hours, you place in the pot a tripod holding a dish on which is lying your chicken, which has had very thin slices of truffles inserted under its skin and which has had a wineglass of Marsala poured into the carcass. In this way the chicken does not touch the liquid and is cooked *au vapeur* from one to one and a quarter hours, according to the size of the chicken. You close the pot hermetically by twisting tightly a damp cloth round the lid. In this way the chicken absorbs the aroma from the meat, vegetables, and herbs, and is tender *à souhait*.

"Exactness in cooking," Dumaine reminded us after this memorable meal, "is difficult to achieve. Generally speaking, you will find that those who don't know how to cook try to make complicated dishes, and vice versa." And then Dumaine came out with the profound remark, *"La grandeur, l'âme de la cuisine, est la simplicité* [the greatness, the soul of cooking, is simplicity]."

"People nowadays," said Dumaine glumly, "seem to be losing the art of simple cooking." I suggested that this was doubtless due to the fact that it requires both patience and experience in perfecting even the humble dishes, such as a Purée de Pommes de Terre.*

"How right you are," he replied, "and when I think of the wonderful things my mother could do with potatoes. What a mess people can make of vegetables. If only they would take a little more interest in what they were doing in the kitchen then the result would be altogether a happier one. Happy, indeed, is the man who owns a small garden where he can pick, fresh, all the herbs he requires for a Court Bouillon.* And that, of course, goes for vegetables too.

"In principle, I am against the use of modern kitchen gadgets. As far as I myself am concerned, nothing today can replace the old-fashioned sieve for making mashed potatoes.* Because they claim they have not time enough for cooking, many prefer laborsaving devices. But my answer is that cooking is not just a matter of pressing buttons. One should forget the gadgets and the tricks and concentrate on

> The Fingers for Working
>
> The Brain for Judging
>
> The Eyes for Seeing
>
> The Nose for Smelling
>
> The Palate for Tasting . . ."

Here are six recipes given to me by Dumaine. Three of them are of vegetable dishes and could not be simpler:

Soup:	Velouté de Grouse Saint-Hubert (serves 6).
Entrée:	Pommes de Terre au Lard (serves 4).
Vegetable Dishes:	Purée de Pommes de Terre (serves 4).
	Petits Pois Paysanne (serves 4).
	Haricots Verts Fins à l'Anglaise (serves 4).
Fowl:	Poulet de Ferme Etuvé à la Digoinaise (serves 4).

VELOUTE DE GROUSE SAINT-HUBERT
(CREAM OF GROUSE SOUP)

Serves 6

1 *plump grouse*	*Mirepoix:*
8 *cups water*	2 *carrots*
3 *broad strips bacon rind*	2 *shallots*
8 *tablespoons butter*	2 *tablespoons celery*
1 *cup lentils*	¼ *cup bacon, blanched*
½ *cup rice*	*Sprig thyme*
Salt, pepper	¼ *bay leaf*

Cookbooks are inclined to go into complicated details for the preparation of velouté soups, especially if game is involved. But here Dumaine shows again that a wonderful result can be obtained by using a simplified cooking process.

Roast the grouse in a very hot oven for about 18 minutes. Remove at once and allow to get cold, then carve carefully all the white meat from the bird, also the meat from the legs (which will be undercooked). Cut up the rest of the bird and make a game stock with the carcass and the bones and the rest of the meat in 8 cups of water (which, in cooking, will reduce to about 6 cups) with the bacon rind and 4 tablespoons of butter; salt and pepper.

Meanwhile, prepare a mirepoix by cutting up the vegetables and the bacon (blanched) into small dice and cooking them gently, with the herbs, in a small open casserole in 2 tablespoons of butter until the vegetables are soft. Remove the mirepoix and place in a pot large enough to hold the game stock. Add the lentils (which should have been soaked in water for two hours) and the rice; also the meat from the legs of the bird. Pour in the stock and simmer gently for one hour, after which time pass the contents of the pot through a fine sieve. Reheat and rectify the seasoning. Add 2 tablespoons of butter and, just before serving, the white meat from the grouse cut up into thin julienne strips.

POMMES DE TERRE AU LARD
(POTATOES WITH BACON)

Serves 4

¾ pound bacon strips
¼ cup butter
16 baby onions
1 tablespoon flour
1½ cups warm water

2 pounds potatoes, sliced
Bouquet garni
Salt, pepper
8 chipolata sausages
Parsley

Brown the bacon strips (which should not be too salty) in
the butter in a casserole, preferably an earthenware one.
Remove and keep warm. Do likewise with the onions. Make a
roux with the flour. Pour in the water. Mix well. Add the
potatoes, the bacon, the onions, the bouquet garni, and salt
and pepper. Cook for about 35 to 40 minutes. Grill the
sausages and keep warm. When the potatoes are cooked, remove the bouquet garni, and arrange them on a hot serving
dish with the bacon, the onions and sausages, and sprinkle
with parsley.

PUREE DE POMMES DE TERRE
(MASHED POTATOES)

Serves 4

2 pounds potatoes
¼ cup butter
¾ cup scalded milk

1 tablespoon fresh cream
Salt, pepper

If the potatoes are large ones, then cut them in half, or in
quarters. Cook them in salted water; the water should cover
them and little more. They must not boil too rapidly, and as
soon as they are cooked, after 20 to 25 minutes, remove and
drain them at once. Replace over a low flame so as to evaporate
the surplus water.

Pass the potatoes through a sieve. It is important that they should be mashed vertically. *Dumaine insists that they should never be put through a vegetable mill, or mashed in a machine with a rotary movement, for this will tend to give the potatoes a stringy and elastic consistency.*

Add the softened butter, piece by piece, to the potatoes, beating vigorously all the time with a wooden spoon. Then gradually add the milk, stirring all the time. Finally add the cream. Salt and pepper to taste and serve at once.

Mashed potatoes is a dish that does NOT improve on being reheated. If these potatoes are to be served to someone with a delicate stomach, then Dumaine recommends that, instead of adding milk to the purée, a mixture of half hot milk and half the hot water in which the potatoes have cooked, should be beaten into the potatoes which will be every bit as pleasant to taste.

PETITS POIS PAYSANNE
(FRESH GREEN PEAS)

Serves 4

4 pounds fresh, unshelled peas	Butter "as large as an egg"
	½ teaspoon powdered sugar
4 small spring onions	Bouquet garni
4 tablespoons water	Salt

Shell the peas, which, says Dumaine, "should be gathered in the garden at eleven o'clock to be eaten at lunchtime."

Place them along with the other ingredients in a casserole, preferably an enamel or an earthenware one. Cover with a soup plate filled with water. Cook gently for 15 to 20 minutes.

HARICOTS VERTS FINS A L'ANGLAISE
(FRENCH BEANS A L'ANGLAISE)

Serves 4

1½ pounds French beans	1 tablespoon butter
Salt, pepper	Parsley

Plunge the beans into a pan containing a large quantity of boiling salted water. As soon as the beans are cooked, which will take about 15 minutes, and are still quite firm (*croquants,* they say in French), remove at once and drain them. Place in a hot serving dish, season with salt and pepper, and place a tablespoon of fresh butter in the middle of them. Sprinkle over them a little fresh parsley cut with scissors and serve immediately.

The secret of succeeding with French beans is that they should be absolutely fresh, picked only an hour or two before cooking, if possible. Dumaine also stresses the importance of the cooking time. They should remain firm, being just cooked and no more. The butter used must be of a superior quality. And the parsley must be cut with scissors, not chopped with a knife. Do not throw away the water in which the beans have cooked as it is excellent for adding to vegetable soups.

POULET DE FERME ETUVE A LA DIGOINAISE
(CHICKEN A LA DIGOINAISE)

Serves 4

¼ cup butter	1½ tablespoons flour
1 farmyard chicken of 2¼ pounds	¾ cup dry white wine
	1 cup water
1 small fresh-water eel of ½ pound	Bouquet garni
	2 cloves garlic
Salt, pepper	

Dumaine describes this regional dish, from Lower Burgundy, as "a traditional dish of the generation of our fathers." "*Nous*

le dégustons avec émotion, assez fréquemment," he says. The
eel binds and gives a surprising smoothness to the sauce.

Melt the butter in a sautoir. Cut the chicken up into 6 or
8 portions and slice the eel. Place eel and chicken in the
sautoir, season with salt and pepper, cover securely and cook
gently for 10 minutes. Turn the pieces of chicken and eel,
cover and cook again, gently, for another 10 minutes.

Remove the chicken and the eel and keep hot. Add the
flour to the juice in the pan, to make a roux, over a low flame.
Stir well. Do not allow to color. Add the wine and the water,
binding the sauce with a whisk. Replace the chicken and the
eel in the sautoir. Add the bouquet garni and the garlic. Cover
and simmer for about 50 minutes over a low flame.

Brown a few pieces of bread, preferably the coarser, country
bread, in a frying pan. Place the pieces of chicken and eel on
top of the bread in a hot serving dish. Pour over the sauce from
the sautoir and serve very hot.

Chez Nous

As indicated in the Foreword, these fifty-six recipes have been selected from our own repertoire of dishes that we prepare in our Paris kitchen. These comprise economical dishes both for the family and for informal lunch and dinner parties. They are all easy to prepare; the sauces, also, that accompany some of them.

Apart from the soups for eight to ten persons, there are "laborsaving" stews, i.e. they constitute dishes pre-prepared for more than one meal and, it will be found, to everybody's satisfaction, that most of them *improve* on being re-heated.

Among the fish dishes, I have selected the commoner, inexpensive kind of fish, in addition to those (also cheap) that are often overlooked in the fish market, but which are delicious and of a fine quality in their own way, especially when appropriately prepared, such as John Dory, gurnet, and sea bream.

I have avoided giving recipes which require time in the making of pastry. This also applies to desserts. Those that appear here are prepared in no time for they entail practically no cooking.

Soups:

> Potage Fermière à la Volaille (serves 10).
> Soupe à l'Oignon Gratinée (serves 3 to 4).
> Potage Purée de Pommes de Terre et
>   Poireaux (serves 10).
> Soupe à la Tomate (serves 6 to 8).

Hors d'Oeuvre:

    Crudités, Sauce Bagnarotte (serves 4).

    Figues au Jambon Fumé (serves 4).

Egg Dishes:

    Oeufs Brouillés "Surprise" (serves 2).

    Oeufs Bigarade (serves 2).

    Oeufs Brouillés Portugaise (serves 2).

    La Piperade (serves 2).

    Chakchouka (serves 4).

Fish:

    Filets de Turbot à l'Indienne (serves 4).

    Filets de Maquereaux à la Bretonne (serves 4).

    Colin Froid, Sauce Mayonnaise (serves 4).

    Cabillaud au Gratin (serves 6).

    Filets de Daurade Pannés à l'Anglaise (serves 4).

    Filets de Saint-Pierre, Sauce Hollandaise
      (serves 4).

    Ecrevisses Scandinave (serves 4).

Fowl:

    Poulet Flambé (serves 4).

    Poule au Pot (serves 5).

    Croquettes de Volaille à la Duchesse (serves 6).

Meat:

    VEAL

    Epaule de Veau aux Oignons (serves 4).

    Pot-au-Feu à la Langue de Veau (serves 4).

      Langue de Veau froide, Sauce Piquante (serves 4).

      Croquettes Grand'mère (serves 4).

    Rognonnade de Veau Printanière (serves 4).

    Sauté de Veau Marengo (serves 6).

    Foie de Veau aux Raisins Secs (serves 6).

BEEF

>Pot-au-Feu Alexandre (serves 6 to 8).
>Steak Tartare (serves 1).
>Boeuf Danois (serves 8).
>Steak Moyen Age (serves 2).

MUTTON

>Navarin de Mouton (serves 4).
>Coeurs d'Agneau Farcis (serves 4).
>Côtes d'Agneau Grillées à la Provençale (serves 2).

PORK

>Porc à l'Orange (serves 6).
>Curry à l'Indo-Chinoise (serves 6).

Vegetable Dishes:

>Pommes Pont-Neuf: *see* Filets de Daurade Pannés à
>l'Anglaise
>Choux de Bruxelles à la Polonaise (serves 4).
>Chou-fleur au Gratin (serves 4).
>Chou Farci (serves 8).
>Riz Créole: *see* Curry à l'Indo-Chinoise

Salads:

>Salade Chinoise (serves 4).
>Salade des Orfèvres (serves 4).
>Salade Fi-Fi (serves 4).

Desserts:

>Riz à l'Amande (serves 12).
>Bananes sur Toast (serves 4).
>Mousse au Citron (serves 6).
>Mousse au Café (serves 6).

Soups

POTAGE FERMIERE A LA VOLAILLE
(CREAM OF VEGETABLE AND CHICKEN SOUP)

Serves 10

Giblets and bones and carcass of a cooked chicken (bone from a cooked leg or shoulder of mutton)
6 pints water
3 leeks, sliced
3 large potatoes, sliced

4 tablespoons butter
3 turnips, sliced
5 carrots, sliced
1 large onion, sliced
4 tender leaves of cabbage, chopped
Salt, pepper

Make a stock for the soup by boiling the chicken giblets and the bones, on which there is some meat left, in 6 pints of boiling, salted water, in a large pot, for one hour. If you happen to have some mutton bones, then add them to the pot.

Take out the bones and remove every little piece of meat from them, chop finely, and reserve. Cut away the top green part of the leeks, wash them thoroughly, and tie in a bundle. Place in the pot along with the sliced potatoes, cover, and simmer for one hour.

Meanwhile, melt the butter in a casserole and place in it the rest of the vegetables, salt, and pepper, and cover securely. Place over a very low flame and cook gently for 15 minutes, or until the vegetables start to soften, then add them to the liquid in the pot, lower flame, and simmer, covered, for another quarter of an hour. Take out the bundle of green leek leaves and discard, and remove carefully all the other vegetables from the pot. Make a purée of them—in an electric beater if you have one—and return to the pot. Stir well, add the chopped chicken (and mutton) meat, cover, and bring gently to a boil. Serve at once.

SOUPE A L'OIGNON GRATINEE
(ONION SOUP AU GRATIN)

Serves 3 to 4

1½ cups onions, chopped
2 tablespoons butter
1 quart consommé or chicken
    bouillon (or water)
Salt, pepper

1 tablespoon port wine
1 egg yolk
Toasted bread
½ cup grated cheese (Parmesan and/or Gruyère)

Soften the onions gently in the butter: they must not color.
Pour in the consommé or the bouillon and season with salt
and pepper. Cover and simmer for 20 minutes. Remove and
pour into an earthenware pot, or an ovenproof casserole. Add
the port beaten with the yolk of the egg. Stir well. Place the
pieces of toasted bread on the surface of the soup. Sprinkle
with the cheese and place in the oven till nicely browned.
Serve very hot straight from the pot or the casserole.

POTAGE PUREE DE POMMES DE TERRE ET POIREAUX
(CREAM OF POTATO AND LEEK SOUP)

Serves 10

2 carrots, sliced
2 onions, sliced
1 stick celery, sliced
4 tablespoons butter
2 pounds leeks, sliced
6 pints consommé or chicken
    bouillon (or water)

Knucklebone of veal, split
1½ pounds potatoes, sliced
Salt, pepper
2 bay leaves
Handful chopped fresh parsley
5 tablespoons fresh cream

Soften the carrots, onions, and celery, in 2 tablespoons butter,
in a large pot. They must not color. Add the leeks. Mix well

together, then add 2 more tablespoons butter. When the leeks are soft pour in the consommé or the bouillon (or water) and add the knucklebone. Bring to a boil and add the potatoes, a little rock salt, and freshly ground pepper, also the bay leaves. Cover, lower the heat, and cook gently for three quarters of an hour. Five minutes before removing from the fire, add the parsley.

Remove the bay leaves and the knucklebone. Pass the soup through a vegetable mill or, better still, make a purée in the electric beater. Replace the bay leaves and the soup in the pot, cover and boil gently for another 10 minutes. Serve with ½ tablespoon of fresh cream in each soup plate.

SOUPE A LA TOMATE
(TOMATO SOUP)

Serves 6 to 8

2 carrots, chopped

2 onions, chopped

2 tablespoons butter

2 tablespoons flour

2 pounds tomatoes, peeled and quartered

2 quarts warm water

Salt, pepper

1 teaspoon sugar

Parsley

½ cup vermicelli

Soften the onions and the carrots in the butter. Add the flour to make a roux. Add the tomatoes. *Tomatoes, like almonds, will peel easily if immersed in boiling water for 2 minutes.* Pour in the warm water. Bring to the boil. Season with salt and pepper and add the sugar and a handful of freshly chopped parsley. Cover and cook gently for three quarters of an hour. Add the vermicelli and simmer for another quarter of an hour. Add about a teaspoon of fresh butter to each plate just before serving.

Hors d'Oeuvre

CRUDITES, SAUCE BAGNAROTTE
(RAW SPRING VEGETABLES WITH SAUCE BAGNAROTTE)

Serves 4

This is a refreshing summer dish, full of vitamins, which you can also serve, by way of a change, at your cocktail parties. It consists of a large platter of raw spring vegetables—cauliflower, celery, carrots, radishes, etc., which you eat with the fingers after dipping them in:

SAUCE BAGNAROTTE

6 *tablespoons Mayonnaise**   1 *teaspoon cognac*
2 *tablespoons tomato ketchup*   *Dash of Tabasco (optional)*
2 *teaspoons fresh cream*   *A few drops of lemon juice*
1 *teaspoon Worcestershire*   *Very little salt and pepper*
  sauce

Mix all the ingredients well together and serve cold along with the platter of neatly arranged raw spring vegetables.

FIGUES AU JAMBON FUME
(FIGS WITH SMOKED HAM)

Serves 4

8 *figs, ripe but not too soft*   *Tissue-thin slices of raw*
                                     smoked ham

Peel the figs carefully. Wrap each one in slices of the raw smoked ham. Leave in the refrigerator just to chill before serving.

Egg Dishes

OEUFS BROUILLES "SURPRISE"
(SCRAMBLED EGGS "SURPRISE")

Serves 2

2 *lamb kidneys*	1½ *tablespoons butter*
Salt, pepper	2 *slices toast*
5 *eggs*	

You cannot fail with scrambled eggs if you cook very fresh country eggs and best quality table butter in a small copper casserole using a wooden spoon to stir them.

Soak the split kidneys in a little water and a teaspoon of vinegar for 10 minutes. Remove and dry, salt and pepper, and grill for 6 or 7 minutes only. *They should be slightly pink inside. Longer cooking will tend to make them leathery.*

As soon as you have started to grill the kidneys, beat the eggs lightly. Salt and pepper slightly. Melt one tablespoon butter in a small copper casserole and pour in the eggs. Stir constantly, with a wooden spoon, over a very low flame, making sure the eggs do not stick to the bottom of the casserole. As soon as the scrambled eggs have reached the desired consistency, remove from the fire and at once incorporate the remaining ½ tablespoon butter in small pieces. *You must do this very quickly for the eggs will continue cooking as long as they remain in the copper casserole.*

Have a piece of toast ready on two plates. Place a kidney on top of each and pour over the scrambled eggs so that the kidneys are hidden. Serve at once.

OEUFS BIGARADE
(EGGS WITH ORANGES)

Serves 2

1 *orange*	1 *teaspoon orange juice*
*Sauce Tomate**	1 *teaspoon lemon juice*
1 *tablespoon Grand Marnier*	4 *fresh eggs*
liqueur	*Salt, pepper*

Peel the outer rind of the orange and blanch in boiling water for 2 minutes. Leave to cool, then cut into thinnest possible julienne strips. Reserve. Remove the inner rind of the orange and cut into four thick, even slices. Reserve.

Prepare the:

SAUCE TOMATE

1 *onion, chopped*	*Flour*
Freshly ground pepper	½ *cup chicken broth or*
Salt	*bouillon*
6 *tomatoes, peeled, seeded,*	*Bouquet garni*
and chopped	1 *tablespoon butter*

Soften the onion in a small pan. Add pepper and salt and the tomatoes. Sprinkle with a little flour (less than a teaspoon), pour in the broth or bouillon, add the bouquet garni, and cook very gently, uncovered, over a low flame until almost all the liquid has disappeared from the pan. Remove the bouquet garni and strain through a fine sieve. Reheat with a walnut-size piece of butter.

Pour the Grand Marnier liqueur and the orange and lemon juice into the hot tomato sauce and mix well. *You can do this over a very low flame, but be careful it does not get too hot otherwise the sauce will start to turn.*

Keep the sauce hot while you cook 4 soft-boiled eggs. Place the 4 slices of orange in a hot, buttered serving dish and on top place the 4 shelled, slightly salted and peppered, soft-boiled eggs. Sprinkle them with the very fine julienne of orange. Pour the sauce over the eggs and serve at once.

OEUFS BROUILLES PORTUGAISE
(SCRAMBLED EGGS WITH TOMATOES)

Serves 2

4 *medium-sized firm tomatoes*   1½ *tablespoons butter*
5 *eggs*   *Salt, pepper*

Peel the tomatoes by plunging them into boiling water for
2 minutes. Drain them thoroughly of their water and chop
them coarsely. Place in a small pan over a low flame, so as to
evaporate the remaining water.

Meanwhile, scramble the eggs as for Oeufs Brouillés "Sur-
prise."* When cooked, place on a hot serving dish and top
with the purée of tomatoes.

LA PIPERADE
(SCRAMBLED EGGS BASQUAISE)

Serves 2

2 *tablespoons butter*   1 *clove garlic, finely chopped*
1 *tablespoon oil*   4 *tomatoes, peeled, seeded,*
½ *cup diced bacon*   *and chopped*
4 *fresh green peppers, seeded*   *Salt, pepper*
  and cut in squares   4 *eggs*
1 *onion, chopped*

Heat the butter and the oil in a frying pan. Cook the bacon,
green peppers, and onion until soft. Add the garlic and tomatoes. Salt and pepper. Raise the heat and, with a fork,
keep crushing up the tomatoes so as to evaporate their water.
About 2 minutes before the vegetables are cooked, add the
four well-beaten eggs to the pan. Keep mixing with the fork
until the eggs are sufficiently scrambled. Remove and serve
the Piperade at once.

CHAKCHOUKA
(RATATOUILLE WITH EGGS)

Serves 4

*Ratatouille**   4 *eggs*

Prepare a hot Ratatouille. The vegetable mixture should be
well crushed and smooth and not too thick.

Pour into a shallow Pyrex dish. With a soupspoon, make
four hollows in the mixture. Break a fresh egg into each hollow. Place the dish in a hot oven and leave till the eggs are
cooked. Serve straight from the Pyrex dish.

Fish

FILETS DE TURBOT A L'INDIENNE
(CURRIED TURBOT)

Serves 4

½ cup shallots, finely chopped
4 tablespoons butter
Salt, pepper
1½ pounds fillets of turbot
1½ teaspoons curry powder
1 clove garlic, chopped

4 tomatoes, peeled, drained, and coarsely chopped
1 cup dry white wine, warmed
½ cup fresh cream

Soften the shallots in two tablespoons butter. Salt and pepper the fillets of turbot and place them in the bottom of a buttered oven (or Pyrex) dish. Add the curry powder and the garlic to the shallots, mix well, and spread over the fish. Add the tomatoes, dot with small pieces of butter and pour in the wine. Cook in the oven, uncovered, for 10 or 12 minutes, basting frequently. Add the fresh cream and continue basting until the fish is cooked (about 20 minutes in all).

If the sauce is too thin, then remove the fish and keep it hot while you reduce the sauce till it starts to thicken. Do not attempt to add flour as a thickening agent as this will only turn the sauce. Never boil a sauce which has both flour and cream in it, for this will spell disaster.

Arrange the fillets of turbot on a hot serving dish and pour over them the curry sauce. Serve with rice as prepared in first paragraph of recipe for Riz Créole.*

FILETS DE MAQUEREAUX A LA BRETONNE
(COLD MACKEREL A LA BRETONNE)

Serves 4

4 very fresh mackerel, filleted	½ teaspoon wine vinegar
Court Bouillon*	1 teaspoon chopped chives
1 teaspoon tarragon mustard	Salt, pepper
2 egg yolks	3 tablespoons melted butter

Have your fishmonger fillet the mackerel. Poach them in the
Court Bouillon for 6 or 7 minutes. Remove, drain, and arrange
them neatly on a serving dish. Leave to cool.

Prepare the sauce by beating together the tarragon mustard
and the egg yolks. Add slowly the vinegar, the chopped
chives, and salt and pepper. Mix well. Add the warm melted
butter carefully to the mixture, which should have the consistency of a thin mayonnaise sauce. Pour over the cold fish,
sprinkle with a little more chopped chives, and decorate with
parsley.

COLIN FROID, SAUCE MAYONNAISE
(COLD HAKE WITH MAYONNAISE SAUCE)

Serves 4

Court Bouillon*	Sauce Mayonnaise*
4 hake steaks of ¼ pound each	

Start by preparing the:

COURT BOUILLON

2 quarts water, or enough to cover the fish well	2 carrots, quartered
	2 onions, quartered
4 bay leaves	Small handful fresh parsley
1 sprig thyme	½ cup wine vinegar
1½ tablespoons rock salt	Freshly ground pepper

Cook together all the ingredients for the Court Bouillon in a
large casserole. Allow to boil, covered, for three quarters of

an hour. Leave to cool. When cold, add the hake steaks and bring gently to a boil, uncovered. As soon as the Court Bouillon shows signs of boiling, lower the heat at once—as low a flame as possible—and poach the fish very gently for 10 minutes.

Remove the fish, skin and bone it carefully, and leave to cool.

Meanwhile, prepare the:

SAUCE MAYONNAISE

2 very fresh egg yolks
½ teaspoon salt
One or two turns of the pepper mill
Dash of French mustard, to flavor

Juice of half a lemon
Oil (peanut oil is best for mayonnaise)

It is really very easy to make a mayonnaise sauce, using only a plate and a fork, if the two following rules are strictly observed. Both the eggs and the oil must be cold, and of the same temperature. And the oil must be added to the egg mixture, at the beginning, drop by drop, beating constantly.

Mix together, in a plate, the egg yolks, salt, pepper, mustard, and half the quantity of lemon juice. Add the oil drop by drop with the one hand, while beating all the time with the other. Never add more oil until it is entirely absorbed into the mixture. As the sauce thickens you can add a little more oil at a time. Continue pouring and beating until you have acquired the right consistency. When you have obtained a firm mayonnaise, add the rest of the lemon juice to smooth the sauce.

CABILLAUD AU GRATIN
(CODFISH PIE)

Serves 6

This is an economical, light fish pie, ideal for the family.

2 pounds fresh cod (middle cut)	Salt, pepper
	Celery salt
Court Bouillon*	3 tablespoons oil
2 pounds potatoes	Handful freshly chopped
3 tablespoons butter	parsley
¼ cup milk, scalded	Bread crumbs

Poach the cod in the Court Bouillon for 20 minutes. Remove at once and keep warm.

As soon as you place the fish in the cold Court Bouillon and put it on the stove, start boiling the potatoes. When cooked, strain them. Replace in the pan over a low flame so as to evaporate all the water. Pass the potatoes through a sieve and return to the pan. Add the butter, bit by bit, beating vigorously with a wooden spoon. Then gradually pour in the warm milk beating all the time till it has all been incorporated into the purée. Add salt, pepper, and celery salt.

Skin and bone the fish, and, with a fish knife and fork, flake the flesh. Add to the potatoes in the pan. Pour in the oil, add the parsley, and gently mix all together. Butter a hot oval dish or a Pyrex dish that will go into the oven. Carefully empty the fish and potato mixture into it. Spread evenly and sprinkle generously with bread crumbs. Dot with little pieces of butter and brown in the oven. Serve very hot.

Another economical, but more substantial, fish pie can be made with the fillets of six mackerel. Prepare the mashed potatoes as indicated for the Codfish Pie. Meanwhile, flour the fillets of mackerel, salt and pepper them, and fry in 2 tablespoons butter and 2 tablespoons oil. Remove the skin and bones from the fillets and break up the fish coarsely with a fork. Proceed exactly as with the cod and complete the cooking of the pie by browning it in the oven.

FILETS DE DAURADE PANNES A L'ANGLAISE
(FRIED FILLETS OF SEA BREAM)

Serves 4

2 sea bream of 1 pound each   Salt, pepper
Bread crumbs   2 tablespoons butter
Flour   2 tablespoons oil
2 whites of egg

Ask your fishmonger to fillet the fish. Wash and dry them. Mix 3 parts bread crumbs with one part peppered flour. Dip the fillets of fish in the whites of egg beaten with one table-spoon oil and then in the flour and bread-crumb mixture.

Sprinkle a little salt over the bottom of a large frying pan and fry the fish, gently, on both sides in the hot butter and the remaining oil. The salt will prevent the fish sticking to the pan and the oil will prevent the butter from burning.

Serve with Pommes Pont-Neuf.*

POMMES PONT-NEUF

4 large potatoes   Salt
Cooking fat or oil

Peel and wash the potatoes and then cut them into equal-sized strips about two inches long and one quarter, or a little more, of an inch thickness. Dry them well, then cook, uncovered, in very hot deep fat or (preferably) oil, for 6 or 7 minutes. Remove the potatoes and drain on absorbent paper. Reheat the fat (or oil) and cook the potatoes again, rapidly, for one or two minutes, or until golden brown and crisp. Remove, dust with fine salt, and serve at once.

FILETS DE SAINT-PIERRE, SAUCE HOLLANDAISE
(FILLETS OF JOHN DORY, WITH HOLLANDAISE SAUCE)

Serves 4

John Dory, an ugly fish whose weight is half made up by its head and bones, is one of the most delicious of fish and especially good with Sauce Hollandaise. Halibut, too, is excellent eaten this way. Reckon a ¼-pound halibut steak per person, for poaching likewise in the Court Bouillon.

2 *pounds filleted John Dory*   *Sauce Hollandaise**
*Court Bouillon**

Start preparing the Hollandaise Sauce at the same moment that you place the fish in the Court Bouillon. As soon as it comes to a boil, the fish should poach for about 15 minutes. Remove at once and keep warm, if, by that time, you have not finished making the sauce.

SAUCE HOLLANDAISE

3 *egg yolks*   *Salt*
1 *teaspoon water*   1 *teaspoon lemon juice*
½ *cup butter*

Place the egg yolks and the water in the top of a double boiler over hot but not boiling water. Whisk until creamy. Add the butter, bit by bit, never putting in one piece until the previous piece has completely disappeared into the sauce. Whisk continuously. Season with a pinch of salt, add the lemon juice and serve immediately with the hot poached fillets of John Dory, accompanied with small new potatoes.

If, in the making of the sauce, it starts to thicken too much, then dilute it with a half teaspoon or more of water. The tricky thing about making Sauce Hollandaise is mostly a matter of heat. You must remove the double boiler from the fire as soon as the sauce thickens enough. If, however, it starts to curdle, then you can rectify this by adding a little boiling water and whisking again to acquire the desired consistency.

ECREVISSES SCANDINAVE
(SCANDINAVIAN CRAYFISH)

Serves 4

4 *dozen crayfish*   10 *tablespoons rock salt*
5 *quarts of water*   8 *tablespoons sugar*
1 *large handful fresh parsley*   1 *teaspoon paprika*
1 *large handful fresh dill*

Wash the crayfish in cold water then plunge them into the boiling water in a large pot containing the herbs and seasoning. Cook for 10 minutes. Remove the pot from the fire and leave the crayfish to cool in the liquid. When cold, remove and place on a large serving dish filled with cracked ice.

Fowl

POULET FLAMBE
(CHICKEN WITH CREAM AND BRANDY SAUCE)

Serves 4

1 *tender roasting chicken*	*¾ cup fresh cream*
Salt, pepper	*Riz Créole**
2 *tablespoons cognac, warmed*	1 *cup butter*

Empty and truss the chicken. Salt and pepper the chicken and brown it quickly on all sides in the butter in a casserole. Then lower the heat and cook gently, covered, for about three quarters of an hour. When it is nearly cooked, remove and cut up and replace in the casserole.

Raise the heat and pour in the warmed cognac and blaze. *If the cognac is poured in cold and the casserole itself is not sufficiently hot then you may not succeed in setting the brandy alight.*

Remove the pieces of chicken, after turning them well around in the juice of the casserole, and keep hot. Add the cream to the juice in the casserole, bring slowly to the boil, reduce the heat and cook very gently, stirring all the time with a wooden spoon, until the sauce starts to thicken. Rectify the seasoning.

Serve the chicken with Riz Créole, making a mound of it in the center of a hot serving dish, and arrange the chicken around it. Serve the sauce separately.

Reserve the giblets, the bones and the carcass for making the Cream of Vegetable and Chicken Soup.*

POULE AU POT
(BOILED CHICKEN WITH VEGETABLES)

Serves 5

1 *young boiling fowl of 3½–4 pounds*
Stuffing
1 *veal knucklebone, split*
3 *quarts consommé, or chicken bouillon (or water)*
3 *onions, two stuck with one clove each*

2 *turnips, diced*
3 *carrots, diced*
1 *stick celery, diced*
5 *leeks, cut into ½-inch strips*
½ *cup barley (optional)*
Bouquet garni
Salt, pepper

STUFFING

1 *cup bread crumbs*
⅓ *cup milk*
Liver and heart of chicken, chopped
¼ *pound sausage meat*
1 *onion, chopped*

1 *clove garlic, chopped*
1 *egg*
1 *teaspoon fresh tarragon leaves, chopped*
Salt, pepper

Reserve the chicken giblets. Prepare the stuffing. First let the bread crumbs soak in the milk, then mix in thoroughly with all the other ingredients for the stuffing. To make the stuffing lighter, add a little water to the mixture. Stuff the chicken and sew it up. Place the chicken, with the neck, wings, feet, gizzard, and the veal knucklebone, in the bottom of a large pot. *A large earthenware marmite, which retains the heat better than any other kind of receptacle, is ideal for cooking this dish.* Add three quarts consommé, or bouillon (or water). Bring to the boil, skim thoroughly, and cook for 10 minutes. Reduce the heat and add the vegetables, the barley, and the bouquet garni. Salt and pepper, cover, and simmer for one and a half hours, or until the chicken is tender.

Remove the chicken. Carve it and serve with the vegetables, a little of the broth, rock salt, and tiny gherkins.

Alternatively, you can serve the chicken with rice and a White Sauce.*

The broth, with the vegetables, makes a delicious soup, especially if you have added the barley.

If you have an ample quantity of chicken and stuffing left over then you can make Croquettes de Volaille à la Duchesse by mixing equal quantities of finely chopped chicken and stuffing with Pommes Duchesse.*

CROQUETTES DE VOLAILLE A LA DUCHESSE
(CHICKEN AND POTATO CROQUETTES)

Serves 6

Pommes Duchesse   *Flour*
1 *pound cooked chicken and*   2 *tablespoons butter*
  stuffing, finely chopped   2 *tablespoons oil*
1 *white of egg*

Make 1 pound of Pommes Duchesse by preparing half of the quantity of Purée de Pommes de Terre* as prescribed by Dumaine. But instead of the milk, substitute 1 egg yolk (reserve the white for coating the croquettes) and 1 tablespoon grated cheese.

Beat the chopped chicken and the stuffing into the Pommes Duchesse and leave to cool, then form into croquettes or rissoles. Dip into the beaten white of egg then roll in flour. Heat the butter and the oil in a large frying pan and brown the croquettes on either side till golden. Serve at once.

Meat

EPAULE DE VEAU AUX OIGNONS
(SHOULDER OF VEAL WITH ONIONS)

Serves 4

1½ pounds shoulder of veal   24 baby onions
Knucklebone of veal, split   Salt, pepper
6 tablespoons butter

Have your butcher cover the sides of the piece of veal with larding pork. *This will prevent the meat from becoming dry in the cooking process.* Heat the butter in a cocotte and as soon as melted add the baby onions and brown them quickly on all sides. Remove and keep warm.

Brown the veal on all sides in the butter in which you have sautéed the onions. Season with salt and pepper. Lower the heat, cover securely, and simmer for three quarters of an hour, after which time add the onions. *When you remove the lid from the cocotte, do so carefully, tipping it so that the water from the steam drips back into the juice in the cocotte.* Continue cooking very gently, and securely covered, for another half an hour. Remove the meat and the onions and keep hot on a serving dish.

Strain the juice from the cocotte through a fine sieve, with a cheesecloth to catch the fat. Reheat the sauce and serve separately, along with Purée de Pommes de Terre.*

If you have inadvertently put too much salt into the mashed potatoes then an extra tablespoon of milk, or cream, will rectify this. A Purée de Pommes de Terre should be eaten as soon as it is cooked. But if your guests are late for dinner then flatten the surface of the mashed potatoes and pour over it a tablespoon of milk, or enough just to cover it. This will prevent a crust forming on top of the potatoes. Cover the pan and keep warm in a bain-marie *(double boiler) or in a slow oven. Just before serving, beat the milk into the potatoes.*

POT-AU-FEU A LA LANGUE DE VEAU
(VEAL TONGUE COOKED IN POT-AU-FEU)

Serves 4

This is what I term a "multipurpose" dish as four separate preparations can be made out of it.

1. Prepare the Pot-au-Feu* as indicated in the recipe, but without the marrow bone, the calf's foot, and the garlic.

Soak a 2–3-pound veal tongue overnight in plenty of cold water. In the morning, drain and wash well. Place the tongue and the knucklebone in the cold water in the pot, bring to the boil, skim thoroughly, reduce the heat, and boil gently for a quarter of an hour. Remove as much of the fat as possible then add all the vegetables and the herbs and the seasoning. Simmer, covered, for an hour and a half, or until tender. Remove the tongue, trim the root end, and take off the skin.

Serve the tongue in the same way as the beef with the drained vegetables arranged neatly around it.

2. You can eat the rest of the tongue cold, or all of it cold, instead of hot, with:

SAUCE PIQUANTE

Salt, pepper	1 *tablespoon freshly chopped*
3 *tablespoons shallots,*	*parsley*
chopped	1 *tablespoon mixed, freshly*
¼ *cup dry white wine*	*chopped, tarragon and*
¼ *cup wine vinegar*	*chives*
1 *cup broth from the Pot-au-*	1 *teaspoon capers*
Feu	1 *small gherkin, sliced*
3 *teaspoons potato flour*	

Salt and pepper the shallots and simmer in the wine and vinegar until reduced by half. Add the broth from the Pot-au-Feu and simmer for another 10 minutes. Thicken with the flour blended with a little of the broth. Mix in gradually, stirring well all the time over a very low flame. Just before serving add the herbs, the capers and the gherkin. Rectify the seasoning. Serve warm.

3. Do not discard the root end of the tongue as this can be used to make delicious, light:

CROQUETTES GRAND'MERE

1 *onion, shredded*	1 *egg*
3 *tablespoons butter*	6 *tablespoons bread crumbs*
½ *pound finely chopped cooked root end of tongue*	*Salt, pepper*
	Flour
½ *pound finely chopped, cooked shoulder of pork*	1 *tablespoon oil*

Soften the onion in a little butter, then mix well together with the tongue, pork, egg, and bread crumbs. Salt and pepper. Gradually add water to the mixture and knead with the hands until you obtain a malleable consistency. *Wet the hands, which will prevent the fingers from becoming sticky and enable you easily and quickly to form croquettes, rolled in flour, of the desired size and shape.* Heat the butter and oil in a frying pan and brown the croquettes on all sides till golden. Serve with a Sauce Tomate.*

4. The Pot-au-Feu, in which the tongue has cooked, makes an excellent and nourishing soup.

ROGNONNADE DE VEAU PRINTANIERE
(SADDLE OF VEAL WITH SPRING VEGETABLES)

Serves 4

Rognonnade de Veau is made from a cut of veal known in France as *longe de veau*. It corresponds to the chump end of loin of veal and is similar to the saddle cut of lamb. Here, on the inner side of the veal cutlets, you will find the kidney.

Have your butcher remove the kidney and cut away most of the outer fat. The *longe* should then be boned, the kidney replaced, and the *bavette,* or flap-end of the cutlets, wrapped around it and the whole rolled and tied for braising.

1½ pounds chump end of loin of veal, with the kidney	12 small onions
½ cup butter	1 cup water
1 cup carrots, sliced	Bouquet garni
	Salt, pepper

Brown the meat in the butter in a stewpan, then add the carrots and the onions. When they, too, are browned, add the warm water and the bouquet garni. Salt and pepper, cover and cook very gently for about one and a quarter hours, or until the veal is tender. *You can tell when the meat is sufficiently cooked by pricking it with the sharp end of a kitchen knife. If a drop or two of clear liquid oozes out of the meat, then it is cooked enough.*

Garnish with new potatoes and hearts of artichokes; spinach; or spring vegetables.

SAUTE DE VEAU MARENGO
(VEAL STEW WITH TOMATOES)

Serves 6

2½ pounds breast of veal	¼ cup flour
Salt, pepper	1 cup dry white wine
2 tablespoons butter	1 cup consommé or bouillon
2 tablespoons oil	1 clove garlic, finely chopped
6 medium-sized onions	Bouquet garni
6 large tomatoes, peeled, seeded, and quartered	½ cup sliced mushrooms
	Chopped parsley

Cut the meat up into 1½-inch cubes. Salt and pepper them and brown in the hot butter and oil, in a saucepan, along with the onions. Add the tomatoes and then the flour to make a roux. Warm the white wine and the consommé, or bouillon (or water) and add to the saucepan, along with the garlic and the bouquet garni. Cover and simmer gently for three quarters of an hour. Add the sliced mushrooms, cover, and simmer for another quarter of an hour. Serve with Riz Créole* and with chopped parsley sprinkled over the meat.

FOIE DE VEAU AUX RAISINS SECS
(CALF'S LIVER WITH RAISINS)

Serves 6

Salt, pepper	Pinch of brown sugar
6 slices of calf's liver	2 tablespoons Madeira
2 tablespoons flour	Soak in warm water for 3
3 tablespoons butter	hours:
1 tablespoon wine vinegar	¼ cup light raisins
¼ cup bouillon	¼ cup dark raisins

Salt and pepper and dredge the slices of liver in flour. Turn them quickly in the hot butter in a frying pan. Remove and place in a buttered Pyrex dish in a warm oven.

Add a half tablespoon of flour to the butter in the frying pan and mix in well, scraping the bottom of the pan, with a wooden spoon. As soon as the butter and the flour start to color, pour in the vinegar and then the bouillon. Add the pinch of brown sugar and boil rapidly for 1 or 2 minutes. Remove the pan from the fire and pour in the Madeira. Stir and then pass the sauce through a fine sieve with a damp cheesecloth. Return the sauce to a small casserole. Add the raisins and heat the sauce, but be careful that it does not boil.

Pour the sauce over the slices of liver and serve with new potatoes.

POT-AU-FEU ALEXANDRE
(BOILED BEEF WITH VEGETABLES)

Serves 6 to 8

2 *pounds shin of beef*	1 *pound turnips, cut and*
½ *calf's foot*	*sliced*
1 *knucklebone of veal*	½ *pound celeriac, cut and*
1 *marrow bone of beef*	*sliced*
8 *pints of water*	4 *onions, three stuck with one*
1½ *pounds of leeks, cut into*	*clove each*
1-*inch slices*	*Bouquet garni*
1½ *pounds of carrots, sliced*	1 *tablespoon rock salt*
2 *cloves garlic, chopped*	*Freshly ground pepper*

Pot-au-Feu is one of the national dishes of France. It is a perfect dish for a large family and is economical and easy to prepare.

Ask your butcher to tie up the piece of meat and to leave a length of string attached. This is to enable you to pull out the meat from the bottom of the pot, instead of fishing for it among the bones and vegetables.

Blanch the calf's foot and the knucklebone in boiling salted water for 10 minutes. Remove and rinse well. Place the beef, with the length of string hanging outside the pot, the calf's foot, and the knucklebone in the pot. Add the marrow bone. Pour in the water and bring to a boil. Skim thoroughly. Lower the heat, cover, and boil over a medium flame for one hour. *Skim off all the fat. An effective way of doing this is to sprinkle cold water on the surface of the liquid in the pot. You will then see the fat rise to the top. Or else, you can leave the Pot-au-Feu in a cool place overnight. By the morning, the fat will have formed a cake which can be easily and quickly removed.*

Put the Pot-au-Feu back on the stove. Add the carrots, turnips, and celeriac. Bring to a boil, then lower the heat. After a quarter of an hour, add the leeks and the onions, and the garlic, the bouquet garni, salt and pepper. Cover and simmer for two and a half to three hours.

Pull out the meat with the aid of the string, slice and place on a hot serving dish with the vegetables arranged around it. Serve with boiled potatoes, gherkins, and horseradish.

Replace in the pot what is left of the meat. This Pot-au-Feu improves as it is progressively reheated. The soup is most nourishing and the last plateful of it is the best of all!

STEAK TARTARE

Serves 1

The secret of a really good Steak Tartare is that the meat should be very fresh and eaten as soon as possible after it has been minced.

¼ *pound tender rump steak,*   ½ *tablespoon tomato ketchup*
  finely minced   1 *teaspoon olive oil*
1 *egg yolk*   *Dash Worcestershire sauce*
1 *teaspoon capers*   *Dash Tabasco*
1 *tablespoon raw chopped on-*   *Salt, pepper*
  ions
½ *tablespoon chopped fresh*
  parsley

Have your butcher mince the meat very finely. Make a flat round of the raw meat in the middle of a plate. With a spoon, make a hollow on top and in it place the raw egg yolk. Around the meat, arrange the capers and the chopped onions and parsley.

Bring to the table and mix well together, and season to taste, with all the other ingredients.

BOEUF DANOIS
(BEEF STEW)

Serves 8

2½ pounds shin of beef	1 knucklebone, split
1½ cup onions, sliced	5 bay leaves
½ cup butter	Warm water
Salt, pepper	Red wine (optional)
2 marrow bones	4 tablespoons flour

This is a simplified Danish version of the well-known Boeuf Bourguignon. It is very easily prepared, is economical (the cut of beef is a cheap one) and is excellent when reheated.

With a very sharp kitchen knife, remove all fat and gristle from the meat. Cut into cubes and *beat each piece of meat with a heavy flat instrument so as to make it more tender for cooking.*

Soften the onions in the butter in a stewpan. Remove and reserve. Brown the cubes of meat in the same butter. Season slightly with salt and pepper. Return the onions to the pan. Add the split knucklebone and the two marrow bones to either ends of which pat in just a little rock salt. *This will prevent the marrow from escaping out into the stew during the cooking process.*

Add the bay leaves and pour in sufficient warm water to cover the meat and the bones. Cover, lower the heat, and simmer for two hours. Remove the knucklebone and pour in red wine to taste. Cover and simmer for another hour.

Remove the pan from the fire. Make a paste with the flour and a little cold water and stir into the stew very gently and slowly, stirring well all the time. Replace the pan on the fire, cover, and bring back slowly to the boil. Simmer for quarter of an hour, then remove the marrow bones. (Marrow, on toast, makes a very good savory.)

Serve the stew straight from the pan accompanied with Mashed Potatoes (Purée de Pommes de Terre).*

STEAK MOYEN AGE
(MEDIEVAL STEAK)

Serves 2

This recipe originates from medieval Flanders. It is a winter
dish and required to be cooked over a log fire. It makes an
excellent and pleasantly different barbecued steak.

1 *thick fillet steak for two*   *Rosemary*
persons

Do *not* salt the steak but merely press, with the heel of the
hand, plenty of rosemary into the flesh of the steak on either
side. Place in a greased folding wire broiler with a long handle
and grill over the glowing embers on either side—3 to 4 minutes on either side should be sufficient to cook it medium-to-
rare. The herb will sputter and crackle over the heat and its
aroma will sink into the meat. As soon as the steak is sufficiently grilled remove the rosemary still adhering to the meat
and place at once on very hot plates. Serve with Pommes Pont-
Neuf.

NAVARIN DE MOUTON
(MUTTON STEW)

Serves 4

2 *pounds shoulder of mutton,*   *Bouquet garni*
boned   1 *cup carrots, diced*
2 *tablespoons butter*   1 *cup turnips, diced*
Salt, pepper   15 *baby onions*
Pinch of sugar   1 *clove garlic, crushed*
2 *tablespoons flour*   12 *small new potatoes*
Warm water   1 *cup cooked peas*
4 *tomatoes, peeled and seeded*

Have your butcher chop up the shoulder of mutton into pieces
of about 2 ounces each. Brown the meat well on all sides in
the butter in a large cocotte. Season with salt and pepper and

add a pinch of sugar. Add the flour to make a roux. Stir thoroughly and pour in sufficient warm water to cover the meat. Bring to a boil, stir again, and add the tomatoes and the bouquet garni. Cover, reduce the heat, and cook gently for one hour.

Remove the meat and keep hot. Pour the juice in the co-cotte through a fine sieve, into a pan. *Remove as much of the fat as possible by sprinkling the surface of the liquid with cold water and then skimming.*

Return the meat and the liquid to the cocotte (which should have been well rinsed with hot water in order to remove any particles of bone) and add all the vegetables, except the potatoes and the peas. Add the garlic, cover, and simmer for half an hour, then add the potatoes and, a quarter of an hour afterwards, the peas. Turn the contents of the cocotte very carefully with a wooden spoon, cover and simmer for another quarter of an hour.

Serve the Navarin straight from the cocotte. This dish is excellent when reheated.

COEURS D'AGNEAU FARCIS
(STUFFED LAMBS' HEARTS)

Serves 4

4 *lambs' hearts*	2 *tablespoons butter*
Salt, pepper	1 *tablespoon flour*
Parsley	*Powdered sugar*

Clean the hearts and soak them in cold water to rinse out the clotted blood inside. Dry them and salt and pepper them in-side and then stuff them with plenty of fresh parsley, not chopped but which has simply had the stalks removed.

Brown the hearts well on all sides in the butter in a small casserole. Pour over sufficient warm water to come up to two thirds of the level of the hearts. Cover securely and simmer for one hour. Remove and skim off the fat. Make a paste of

the flour and a little water and pour in gently, stirring well all
the time. Put back on the fire, rectify the seasoning, and add
a pinch of sugar. Cover and simmer for quarter of an hour.
Serve with new potatoes and French Beans.*

COTES D'AGNEAU GRILLEES A LA PROVENCALE
(LAMB CHOPS WITH GRILLED TOMATOES)

Serves 2

4 *firm tomatoes*   *Finely chopped:*
2 *tablespoons butter*   *Chervil*
1 *clove garlic, finely chopped*   *Parsley*
Salt, pepper   4 *lamb chops*

Cut the tomatoes in half horizontally and, with the aid of a
teaspoon, scoop out the water and seeds from each segment
and insert tiny pieces of butter. Sprinkle each tomato with
garlic and a little of the herbs (two portions of chervil to one
of parsley). Salt and pepper slightly and place under the
grill.

While the tomatoes are grilling, cook the lamb chops. Do
not salt them before placing on the grill. As soon as both are
done serve together at once.

PORC A L'ORANGE
(PORK WITH ORANGE)

Serves 6

3 *pounds loin of pork*   *Bouquet garni*
3 *tablespoons butter*   4 *carrots, diced*
Salt, pepper   ½ *cup dry white wine*
2 *tablespoons cognac,*   ½ *cup chicken bouillon*
  warmed   2 *oranges*
1 *knucklebone of veal*   *Arrowroot*

Brown the meat on all sides, in the butter, in a cocotte. Salt
and pepper. Pour in the cognac and blaze. Add the knuckle-

bone of veal, the bouquet garni, and the carrots. Pour in the white wine and the bouillon, cover and simmer for one and a half hours, or until the pork is tender.

Meanwhile, take two oranges. Peel the rind of both and blanch in boiling water for 2 minutes. Remove and leave to cool and then cut into the thinnest possible julienne strips. Squeeze out the juice from one of the oranges and reserve. Skin the other one and cut into slices and reserve.

When the pork is cooked, remove from the cocotte, along with the carrots, and cut into slices and arrange on a hot serving dish. *Strain the juice in the cocotte through a sieve with a damp cheesecloth, so as to catch the fat,* and pour into a small pan. Add the orange juice and the orange julienne strips. Make a thin paste with a little arrowroot and water and add to the sauce so as to thicken it. Bring to a boil, cook gently for 6 or 7 minutes, stirring well, then pour over the sliced pork. Arrange the slices of orange around the meat and serve at once.

CURRY A L'INDO-CHINOISE
(CURRIED PORK)

Serves 6

2½ pounds boned bladebone of pork	5 cloves of garlic, finely chopped
2 tablespoons butter	Riz Créole*
Salt	Palm shoots
3 tablespoons oil	6 eggs
1 cup onions, chopped	3 firm, medium-sized tomatoes
1½ tablespoons flour	
1 tablespoon curry powder	Juice of a lemon
3 cups warm water	Mango chutney

Cut the meat into cubes and brown quickly on all sides in the butter, in a stewpan. Salt, cover, and keep warm.

Heat the oil in a deep frying pan over a brisk flame, and as soon as it starts to smoke, add the onions. Keep stirring well with a wooden spoon until the onions start to color, then add the flour and the curry powder (a strong Madras curry powder is the best). Lower the heat and pour in one cup warm water. Stir well, and 2 or 3 minutes later, pour in another cup of warm water. After 5 minutes, add a third cup of warm water. Raise the heat so that the liquid comes to a boil. Stir well and pour into the stewpan containing the meat. Add the garlic, bring to a boil, and cook rapidly for 5 minutes; then cover, lower the heat, and simmer very gently for two hours. If the liquid reduces too rapidly, gradually add more hot water. Stir every now and again with a wooden spoon, to prevent the meat sticking to the bottom of the pan.

Meanwhile, prepare the rice:

RIZ CREOLE
(CRÉOLE RICE)

½ tablespoon butter
1½ cups unwashed long-grain rice

3 cups boiling water
Salt

Melt the butter in the bottom of a casserole. *The rice will cook better in a copper casserole which retains an even distribution of heat throughout.* Add the rice and stir, with a wooden spoon, over a medium flame, for about a minute only. Then pour in the boiling water. Add a little salt. Place a folded clean kitchen cloth over the casserole, and on top four plates (for the curry dish). Lower the heat and boil gently for 20 to 25 minutes by which time the water will have disappeared and the rice should be perfectly cooked, with every grain separate. (Leftover Riz Créole may be used in the preparation of Tomates du Midi.*)

Remove the curried pork and serve garnished with palm shoots, fried eggs (*which, to remove easily from the pan with-*

out breaking them, should be lifted out with a kitchen spatula preheated in boiling water) and slices of cold, fresh tomatoes to offset the hot sauce. *If the curry sauce is found to be too strong then whisk a little fresh coconut milk into it.*

This dish can be made to look very attractive if the rice from a ring mold is set in the center of a large, hot serving dish and the curried pork, with the sauce poured over it, placed in the middle of it. Place palm shoots at either end of the dish and, around the ring of rice, alternate slices of tomatoes with fried eggs. Serve the mango chutney separately.

This curry dish improves on being reheated. Remove the top fat, add the juice of a lemon, turn the pieces of meat gently with a wooden spoon, and reheat slowly.

Vegetable Dishes

CHOUX DE BRUXELLES A LA POLONAISE
(BRUSSELS SPROUTS A LA POLONAISE)

Serves 4

2 pounds Brussels sprouts, of equal size
2 or 3 sprigs of parsley
¼ cup cold, crumbled, hard-boiled egg yolks
2 tablespoons freshly chopped parsley
½ cup butter
2 tablespoons bread crumbs

Remove the outer leaves and cut off the hard end of the stalks of the sprouts. Wash well and leave for quarter of an hour in a basin of warm, salted water. Remove and drain thoroughly.

Plunge the sprouts into a large pan of boiling, salted water. *Add the sprigs of (well-washed) parsley which, during the cooking process, will take away some of the bitterness from the sprouts.* Cook, uncovered, for 15 minutes or until the sprouts are just tender (they must not get soft). Remove at once, strain, and place in a hot buttered dish.

Mix together the crumbled egg yolks and the parsley and sprinkle over the sprouts. Heat the butter in a small pan until it starts to turn nut brown. Add the bread crumbs and fry them rapidly. As soon as the butter becomes frothy remove and pour over the sprouts and serve at once.

CHOU-FLEUR AU GRATIN
(CAULIFLOWER AU GRATIN)

Serves 4

1 *cauliflower of about* 3 *pounds*	*½ cup mixed, grated Gruyère and Parmesan cheese*
Salt	*Bread crumbs*
White Sauce*	*Butter*

Detach the flowerlets from the cauliflower, cut off the harder piece from the stalks, and place in a large pan of warm, salted water. Wash and rinse thoroughly, then plunge the flowerlets into large pot of boiling, salted water. Boil, uncovered, for about 8 minutes, or until just cooked (the stalks must remain firm, just giving way to the fingers and no more). Remove from the fire and pour in a glass of cold water. *This will stop the cauliflower from cooking more and enable you to take your time removing the flowerlets carefully and placing them on absorbent paper to drain them of their water.*

Prepare the:

SAUCE BLANCHE
(WHITE SAUCE)

2 *tablespoons butter*	*Salt, pepper*
2 *tablespoons flour*	*Nutmeg*
1½ *cups of scalded milk*	

Make a roux by mixing the hot butter and the flour in a small pan. Stir over a medium flame until it starts to color. Gradually add the milk which should be the same temperature as the roux. When all the milk has been added, lower the flame and simmer for 20 minutes. At the last minute add a teaspoon of butter, a little salt and pepper, and a pinch of grated nutmeg.

Butter an oval Pyrex dish and arrange in it, evenly, the flowerlets of cauliflower. Sprinkle over them half the grated cheese. Pour over the White Sauce, sprinkle again with the rest of the cheese. Cover with bread crumbs, dot with small pieces of butter, and brown in the oven. Serve very hot.

Reserve the water in which the cauliflower has cooked for using in the preparation of soups.

CHOU FARCI
(STUFFED CABBAGE)

Serves 8

2 *pounds shoulder of pork*	1 *large, fresh, white cabbage*
12 *tablespoons bread crumbs*	4 *tablespoons butter*
2 *onions, shredded*	*Pinch of sugar*
1 *egg*	2 *pounds small new potatoes*
Salt, pepper	2 *tablespoons flour*
Water	*Grated nutmeg*

Order two pounds of shoulder of pork from your butcher and get him to trim it of all excess fat and then mince it. Mix well together the meat, the bread crumbs, the onions, and the raw egg. Season with salt and pepper. Gradually add a cup or more of water to the mixture and knead with the hands until you obtain a malleable consistency.

Remove the core of the cabbage and separate the leaves. Place them in a pan and pour over them 2 cups of warm, salted water. Bring to the boil. Press down the leaves of the cabbage until they start to soften. Remove and drain.

Place 2 tablespoons of butter and a cup of water in the bottom of a stewpan, then line it with two thirds of the cabbage leaves. Add a pinch of sugar and a little pepper. Add the pork stuffing, cover with the remaining cabbage leaves. Cover the stewpan and simmer for about three quarters of an hour, or until the cabbage leaves are tender. Meanwhile, cook the potatoes.

Remove and strain off the juice from the dish. Make a roux with the flour and the rest of the butter and slowly add the strained juice to make a White Sauce.* Add a pinch of grated nutmeg to the sauce and, at the last minute, the final juice from the stuffed cabbage. Turn the stuffed cabbage upside down onto a hot dish and serve at once, sliced, with the potatoes and the White Sauce.

If you have some of the pork stuffing left over, then you can use this for making pleasantly light fried meat balls. Miniature size, they are delicious, in soups (reserve the water in which the cabbage has cooked for this purpose). All you need do is to drop them into boiling water for a few minutes. When they rise to the surface, they are sufficiently cooked for placing in the soup tureen.

Salads

SALADE CHINOISE
(CHINESE SALAD)

Serves 4

This is a most refreshing summer salad and is useful for using what is left of the carcass of the cold chicken.

1 *cup soya bean sprouts*
½ *cup chilled New Orleans prawns*
½ *cup diced cooked chicken*
*Sauce Vinaigrette**

1 *fresh, crisp romaine (cos) lettuce, cut in strips*
2 *tomatoes, sliced and quartered*
½ *cup sliced and quartered cucumber*

Wash thoroughly the soya bean sprouts and plunge them into boiling, salted water for just under 1 minute. Remove immediately and dry and chill them.

The New Orleans prawns should be steamed rapidly for about 10 minutes, or until the shells turn red as when cooking lobster. Then shell them, cut into thin slices when cold, and place in the refrigerator along with the diced chicken.

Prepare the Sauce Vinaigrette preferably with the lemon juice and without the tarragon mustard. Pour into a salad bowl. Place in it the vegetables and arrange the chicken and prawns neatly on top. Leave in the refrigerator to chill. Turn the salad at the last minute before serving.

SALADE DES ORFEVRES
(ENDIVE, BEETROOT, AND WALNUT SALAD)

Serves 4

1 cup diced beetroot
½ cup walnuts, halved

¾ pound fresh, firm Belgian
  endive
Sauce Vinaigrette*

Dice the beetroot, halve the walnuts, and wash and dry the
endives and cut into 1½-inch slices.

Prepare the:

SAUCE VINAIGRETTE

4 tablespoons olive or peanut
  oil
1 tablespoon wine vinegar, or
  lemon juice

A little tarragon mustard
Freshly ground pepper
Salt

Mix all the ingredients well together and pour into a salad
bowl. Place in it the endives, beetroot, and walnuts. Leave in
the refrigerator to chill. Bring to the table and turn the salad
in the dressing just before serving.

SALADE FI-FI
(ROMAINE [COS] AND MUSHROOM SALAD)

Serves 4

Sauce Vinaigrette*
1 fresh, crisp romaine (cos)
  lettuce, cut in broad strips

½ cup finely sliced, raw mushrooms
1 tablespoon finely chopped
  mixed chives and parsley

Prepare the Sauce Vinaigrette and pour into the salad bowl.
Place in it the lettuce and, on top, the sliced mushrooms.
Sprinkle with the herbs. Place in the refrigerator to chill. Turn
the salad at the table just before serving.

Desserts

RIZ A L'AMANDE
(RICE AND ALMOND DESSERT)

Serves 12

6 tablespoons rice
2 pints milk
½ stick vanilla, split
¾ ounce powdered gelatin or
  10 gelatin leaves
¼ cup water

¼ cup sugar
3 cups cream
6 tablespoons almonds, peeled
  and chopped
Rum or port wine to flavor

Cook the rice gently in the milk for about three quarters of an hour, with the vanilla stick. Meanwhile, soak the gelatin leaves in cold water. When the rice is cooked, remove from the flame, add the sugar, and leave to cool. Drain the water from the gelatin leaves and melt them very gently (they must not cook) over a low flame. Whip the cream.

Add the melted gelatin to the cold cooked rice. Next add the chopped almonds and the flavoring and stir in very gently so as not to break the grains of the rice.

Add the whipped cream to the dish, mixing it in well and right down to the bottom of the bowl in which it is going to be served, until the whole starts to set. Leave to chill until ready to serve.

BANANES SUR TOAST
(BANANAS ON TOAST)

Serves 4

3 *bananas*
1 *tablespoon butter, softened*
½ *teaspoon lemon juice*

½ *teaspoon salt*
¼ *teaspoon paprika*
4 *slices toast*

Mash the bananas and incorporate the butter, lemon juice, salt, and paprika. Spread evenly over four pieces of toast. Heat under the grill until the surface is slightly browned. Serve at once.

MOUSSE AU CITRON
(LEMON MOUSSE)

Serves 6

5 *eggs*
½ *cup powdered sugar*
1 *cup cream*
½ *ounce powdered gelatin or*
   7 *gelatin leaves*

¼ *cup water*
Juice of 1½ *lemons*

Separate the eggs and beat together the yolks with the sugar until they turn white.

Beat the whites of the eggs till very stiff. Beat the cream till it, too, stiffens. Soak the gelatin in the cold water. Stir the lemon juice into the egg yolks. Drain the water from the gelatin leaves and melt them very gently over a low flame. Stir the melted gelatin gently into the egg-yolk, sugar, and lemon mixture, and when it starts to stiffen fold in, very carefully, the egg whites. Add half the quantity of the cream, mixing gently right down to the bottom of the bowl so that it becomes light and fluffy. Empty into the serving bowl and decorate with the rest of the cream. *The serving bowl should be rinsed with cold water so as to prevent the mousse from sticking to the sides.*

MOUSSE AU CAFE
(COFFEE MOUSSE)

Serves 6

3 *eggs*
½ *cup powdered sugar*
2 *cups cream*
½ *ounce powdered gelatin or*
  5 *gelatin leaves*

¼ *cup water*
½ *cup strong, black,* cold *coffee*

Separate the eggs and beat together the yolks with the sugar until they turn white.

Beat the whites of the eggs till very stiff. Beat the cream till it, too, stiffens. Soak the gelatin in the cold water. Stir cold black coffee into the egg yolks. Drain the water from the gelatin and melt very gently over a low flame. Stir the melted gelatin into the egg-yolk, sugar, and coffee mixture, and when it starts to stiffen fold in, very gently, the egg whites. Be careful not to crush them. Add the cream, stirring very gently, right down to the bottom of the bowl. Keep stirring gently until the mousse starts to stiffen, as the gelatin otherwise will settle in the bottom. Empty into the serving bowl, which should be rinsed with cold water, and decorate with a little cream.

What the Famous Paris Restaurateurs Eat When Alone

Egg Dishes:

Oeufs Parmentier (serves 2).

Oeufs au Beurre Noir (serves 1).

Tomates Lucien (serves 1).

Fish:

Daurade au Gratin (serves 4).

Palets de Morue Vieille Benoîte (serves 6).

Grondin Rôti au Beurre Montpensier (serves 4).

Mouclade d'Esnandes (serves 4).

Fowl:

Poulet Sauté Paysanne (serves 4).

Foies de Volaille André (serves 1).

Meat:

Paupiettes de Boeuf Flamande (serves 6).

Côtes de Veau aux Cèpes (serves 4).

Oreilles et Pieds de Porc aux Haricots Rouges (serves 4).

Rognons de Veau Sautés (serves 4).

Vegetable Dishes:

Beignets de Pommes de Terre (serves 4).

Gnocchi aux Champignons (serves 6).

Poireaux au Gratin (serves 4).

Purée de Pommes de Terre (serves 4).

PART ONE

One day, as I chanced to pass by the *Restaurant Lapérouse,* on the Quai des Grand Augustins, I decided to call in and exchange a few words with the proprietor, *Monsieur Topolinski,* who happens to be one of my neighbors. The time was 12:45 P.M., and I should have remembered that at that hour the illustrious owner of this celebrated establishment would probably be having his lunch. This was the case, for I was conducted to a small back room where I found Monsieur Topolinski enjoying a meal all by himself and with such evident relish that I inquired what it was he was eating. "Potato Pancakes, mon cher, and how I adore them," he answered with a flourish of his fork. "When I am alone I always ask my chef, Monsieur Delorme—who prepares to perfection our great specialties such as Homard Babinski, Canard de Colette, and Poulet Docteur—to cook me something simple. Yesterday, for example, he gave me a Grilled Herring with a Mustard Sauce. Quelle délice! Tomorrow being Friday, I shall ask him for a Daurade au gratin. There's nothing like good, honest, simple fare now and again, especially for us restaurateurs who enjoy *la haute cuisine* just as much as do our gourmet clientèle. But, as I have said, an occasional return to plain, simple cooking is both a necessary and pleasurable change for everyone."

I left the Restaurant Lapérouse wondering what the other well-known Paris restaurateurs ate when alone. Did they, too, enjoy *la cuisine simple* to this extent? The result of my inquiries was most revealing.

Of the eight restaurateurs listed here, whom I visited, the first five are the proprietors of the five existing three-star restaurants in Paris. The others are the proprietors of the next leading great restaurants of the capital.

BEIGNETS DE POMMES DE TERRE
(POTATO PANCAKES)

Serves 4

1¼ *pounds potatoes*	½ *cup grated Parmesan, or*
1 *onion, chopped*	*Gruyère cheese*
1 *tablespoon butter*	½ *cup milk*
2 *eggs*	*Pinch nutmeg*
⅓ *cup flour*	*Salt, pepper*

Peel the potatoes. Wipe them well, but don't wash them. Grate them finely. Soften the chopped onion in the butter. Mix thoroughly together the onion with the potatoes and all the other ingredients.

Butter a small pancake pan, add a teaspoon of oil (which will prevent the butter from burning), and make pancakes of the mixture about the thickness of blinis. Allow about 6 minutes each side. Serve very hot.

DAURADE AU GRATIN
(SEA BREAM POACHED IN WHITE WINE)

Serves 4

2 *sea bream, of ½ pound each*	*Salt, pepper*
½ *cup butter*	2 *cups dry white wine*
½ *cup shallots, chopped*	*Bread crumbs*

If sea bream is not available, then either gray mullet or bass make excellent substitutes, for which the cooking process is just the same.

Place the butter in the bottom of a hot Pyrex dish which will go into the oven. Place in it the chopped shallots. Score the fish lightly on either side. Salt and pepper them and place them on the bed of shallots. Warm the white wine and add to the dish and poach the fish, uncovered, in a medium oven for about 25 minutes, basting frequently. Five minutes before serving, sprinkle the bread crumbs over the fish.

Monsieur Raymond Oliver is the celebrated proprietor of the three-star *Grand Véfour Restaurant*, in the Rue du Beaujolais, at the far end of the gardens of the Palais-Royal. This has always been one of my favorite restaurants, not only on account of the superb cuisine, and its incomparable cellar, but also for the great comfort and the elegance of its setting. The interior is pure Directoire and the atmosphere truly reminiscent of the epoch. Napoleon regularly frequented the Grand Véfour when a young general, and it was at the coffee shop next door that he chanced to meet Joséphine de Beauharnais.

La haute cuisine française is the order of the day at the Grand Véfour, especially when Monsieur Oliver himself takes control of the kitchens. Bearing in mind his famous *spécialités* such as Croûte Landaise, Ortolans aux Raisins, Pigeon Prince Rainier, etc., I humbly inquired if he ever cooked a "simple" dish for himself? "Often," he answered, "and I get a kick out of perfecting an easy recipe such as Poulet Sauté Paysanne,* or a very simple egg dish."

OEUFS PARMENTIER
(EGGS WITH POTATOES)

Serves 2

4 *large potatoes*	*Salt, pepper*
2 *tablespoons butter*	4 *eggs*
1 *tablespoon olive oil*	

Roast the potatoes, in their jackets, in the oven. When they are cooked, cut them in half lengthwise, remove the pulp, and sauté rapidly in the very hot butter and oil. Salt and pepper. Remove to a shallow Pyrex baking dish. Break the eggs over the potatoes and bake in a medium oven until the eggs are just cooked. Serve at once.

POULET SAUTE PAYSANNE
(FRIED CHICKEN)

Serves 4

1 *frying chicken, for 4 persons*
¼ *cup lard*
1 *sprig thyme*
1 *bay leaf*
2 *tablespoons dripping*

1 *tablespoon olive oil*
Salt, pepper
4 *medium-sized onions, quartered*
4 *medium-sized potatoes, quartered*
Chopped parsley

Cut the chicken up, including the carcass, into eight or ten pieces. Place the lard, the thyme, the bay leaf, the dripping, and the oil in a large, deep frying pan and, as soon as it starts to sizzle, add the pieces of chicken and brown them rapidly. Season slightly with salt and freshly ground pepper. Continue to cook, uncovered, for 5 or 6 minutes after which time add the onions and the potatoes. Cook over a fast flame for another 5 or 6 minutes, or until the vegetables and chicken are well browned. Season once more. Cover and cook over a medium flame, for 10 or 12 minutes. Remove the herbs. Sprinkle chopped parsley over the dish and serve at once straight from the pan.

Most American gastronomes who know Paris claim *La Tour d'Argent,* on the Quai de la Tournelle, to be the best and the smartest restaurant in the capital. The proprietor, *Monsieur Claude Terrail,* certainly caters more than any other Paris restaurateur to a regular American V.I.P. clientèle who frequent the restaurant, not only for the superlative cooking (and the famous Pressed Duck that Monsieur Terrail has proudly served to the royalty of Europe) but also for the unique fifth-floor view overlooking the Seine and the apse of Notre-Dame Cathedral.

I have occasionally come across Monsieur Terrail partaking of a very simple meal, around 2:30 P.M., when the restaurant is clearing after the luncheon service. But, apart from succulent steaks, what else did his well-known chef, Monsieur Descreux, sometimes prepare for him by way of bourgeois cooking? My inquiry led to the following two recipes:

PALETS DE MORUE VIEILLE BENOITE
(FISH AND POTATO PANCAKES)

Serves 6

1 *pound salt codfish*	1 *tablespoon fresh cream*
1 *pound potatoes*	2 *tablespoons butter*
1 *teaspoon fines herbes*	*Salt, pepper*
1 *clove garlic*	1 *teaspoon olive oil*
2 *eggs, beaten*	

Leave the fish to soak overnight in plenty of water (place the side with the skin uppermost). In the morning, change the water and allow the fish to soak again for several hours. Then place the cod in a large pan of fresh, cold water. Bring gently to a boil and poach for quarter of an hour.

Meanwhile, roast the potatoes, in their jackets, in the oven. When cooked, peel them and pass them through a fine sieve.

Remove the fish from the pan of water, dry it, and hash it, and then mix it well with the potatoes, the fines herbes, the garlic, the two beaten eggs, the cream, and one tablespoon of melted butter. Season with salt and pepper and beat thoroughly together so as to obtain a paste with which you make small pancakes (size and thickness of blinis pancakes). They should be cooked in oil and one tablespoon of butter until brown on either side.

PAUPIETTES DE BOEUF FLAMANDE
(THIN STUFFED ESCALOPES OF BEEF)

Serves 6

6 *thin escalopes of beef, 4 ounces each, cut from the rump*
Larding pork
6 *tablespoons hashed pork meat*
Fines herbes
½ *cup butter*

3 *onions, chopped*
2 *carrots, cut in strips*
1 *tablespoon tomato purée*
¾ *cup dry white wine*
Bouquet garni
Consommé, or stock
Salt, pepper

Have your butcher flatten the escalopes and give you six strips of larding pork of the same size. Place a tablespoon of pork meat, seasoned with fines herbes, on each escalope and roll in the form of a sausage. Wrap a strip of larding pork around each meat roll and tie securely with fine string.

Brown the rolled escalopes, in a cocotte, in the butter along with the carrots, the onions, and the bouquet garni. Add the white wine and the tomato purée and pour in sufficient consommé (or stock) to cover the meat. Season with salt and pepper. Cover and cook gently for about one hour.

Remove the rolled escalopes and the bouquet garni and cut the strings and carefully take away the larding pork. Keep the escalopes hot while you reduce the sauce in the pan until it starts to thicken. Serve with braised Belgian endives, or rice, or spaghetti, with the rolled escalopes placed in the middle of the dish and the sauce poured over them.

Maxim's, in the Rue Royale, is probably the most famous restaurant in the world. It has been the subject of songs and operettas, and stories about it have been told many times on stage and screen. The restaurant has retained its true turn-of-the-century décor and atmosphere and if, nowadays, it is less "naughty" than during the nineties, it still expresses a charm and gaiety that is quite unique, while the standard of its celebrated cuisine has never varied.

Monsieur Alexandre Humbert is the head chef. He is a fanatic for non-stop work in the kitchens. He makes no point of cooking *spécialités* of his own, for he claims that a truly able chef should be able to prepare any, and all *spécialités!*

Monsieur Louis Vaudable is the very active director of Maxim's. By way of a change from *la haute cuisine française* of his own kitchens he occasionally asks Alexandre Humbert to prepare him as simple a dish as Oeufs au Beurre Noir* or a Côte de Veau aux Cèpes.*

OEUFS AU BEURRE NOIR
(EGGS IN BLACK BUTTER)

Serves 1

2 eggs
1 tablespoon butter

Dash vinegar
1 teaspoon capers

Cook the eggs, in a well-buttered ramekin, in a medium oven until the whites are just about to set. Heat the butter in a small pan and when it starts to turn dark nut-brown in color, remove at once and add the vinegar and capers. Pour the butter and capers sauce over the whites of the eggs and serve at once.

COTES DE VEAU AUX CEPES
(VEAL CUTLETS WITH FLAP MUSHROOMS)

Serves 4

4 *very thin veal cutlets*
2 *tablespoons butter*
2 *tablespoons oil*
1 *pound* cèpes *(canned or bottled flap mushrooms), or 1 pound large ordinary mushroom caps*

1 *tablespoon shallots, chopped*
Salt, pepper
Chopped parsley

Brown the veal cutlets quickly in the hot butter and oil. Lower the heat and cook for 2 or 3 minutes only on either side. Remove from the pan and keep hot. Remove the stalks from the flap mushrooms and add them to the hot pan in which the cutlets have cooked. Sauté until they start to brown then add the shallots and sauté for a few more minutes. Salt and pepper. Add the vegetables to the dish with the veal cutlets, sprinkle with chopped parsley, and serve at once.

Lasserre is a luxurious and very comfortable establishment situated right opposite the Palais de la Découverte, in the Avenue Franklin D. Roosevelt. Many who have wined and dined here for the first time have come away saying that they themselves have made a real discovery in the realm of gastronomy.

Monsieur Lasserre, the proprietor, who was formerly at the famous Prunier and Drouant restaurants, came here shortly before the end of the war and quickly earned success on account of the excellence of his cuisine. An original and striking feature of the restaurant is the formation of the exclusive gastronomic Club de la Casserole which is composed of regular customers at Lasserre who foregather to enjoy the specialties of Monsieur Auguste Perrot, who is in control of the kitchens. This remarkable chef, who has won most of the great culinary prizes of France, takes pleasure in preparing the simplest of dishes for Monsieur Lasserre, such as les Foies de Volaille André* and les Tomates Lucien.*

FOIES DE VOLAILLE ANDRE
(CHICKEN LIVERS WITH ONIONS)

Serves 1

5 *chicken livers*　　　　　*Salt, pepper*
2 *tablespoons butter*　　 *½ cup onions, finely chopped*

Sauté the livers in the butter. Salt and pepper slightly. Add the onions. Season again slightly. Cook for about 10 to 12 minutes. Serve very hot.

TOMATES LUCIEN
(EGGS AND TOMATOES)

Serves 1

3 *medium-sized tomatoes*   *Salt, pepper*
Olive oil   2 *eggs*

Peel the tomatoes and drain them entirely of their water.
Quarter them and cook them for 7 or 8 minutes in a very
little oil, in a frying pan. Season to taste. Remove from the
fire and add the raw, unbeaten eggs and mix in gently with
the tomatoes. As soon as the mixture is cooked, serve at once.

PART TWO

Drouant, on the Place Gaillon, is one of those quiet, but always busy, well-appointed restaurants that are ideal for business lunches. The service is *soigné* and there are numerous
salons particuliers. In one of these, the Jury of the Prix Gon-
court always holds its annual banquet. *Monsieur Jean Drouant*
is the proprietor of this excellent establishment specializing in

seafood. He also owns Fouquet's, on the Champs-Elysées, and the very elegant Pré Catalan restaurant in the Bois de Boulogne.

The cellar Chez Drouant is extremely well stocked and Monsieur Drouant, who is a great connoisseur of wines, is often tasting them to the accompaniment of some new and simple dish. When we lunched with him recently we were given two unusual dishes to try, the Grondin Rôti au Beurre Montpensier* (because the chef, *Monsieur Jules Petit,* wished to experiment with the sauce for this fish) and the Oreilles et Pieds de Porc aux Haricots Rouges,* as this is one of Monsieur Drouant's favorite dishes when not lunching in company.

Here are the two recipes:

OREILLES ET PIEDS DE PORC AUX HARICOTS ROUGES
(PIG'S FEET AND EARS WITH RED BEANS)

Serves 4

¾ pound red beans	4 shallots, chopped
4 ounces salted bacon	1 cup red wine
1 onion, stuck with 2 cloves	2 tablespoons beurre manié
1 carrot, quartered	(two portions of butter to
Bouquet garni	one of flour)
3 cloves garlic	2 pig's ears and 1 foot
10 peppercorns	

Soak the beans overnight. In the morning, drain off the water and add fresh water to the pan to cover the beans. Add the bacon, the onion stuck with two cloves, the carrot, the bouquet garni, and the garlic and the peppercorns enclosed in a small bag. Cook, well covered, for one hour or until the beans are tender.

Remove the bouquet garni and the small bag containing the garlic and the peppercorns. Remove also the bacon and keep warm. Strain the contents of the pan. Cook the chopped shallots gently in the red wine until reduced by half, then add to the beans. Cook the vegetables again, gently, for a quarter of an hour and then bind with the beurre manié.

Meanwhile, blanch the pig's foot for 10 minutes. Remove, rinse well, dry, and braise until tender. Remove the center bone and cut the meat into large pieces. Do likewise with the bacon and then add the foot and the bacon to the beans. Brown in the oven. Remove from the oven and place on top two cooked and quickly grilled pig's ears. Serve very hot.

GRONDIN ROTI AU BEURRE MONTPENSIER
(RED GURNARD WITH HERB BUTTER)

Serves 4

4 red gurnard, or red mullet of 7 ounces each	Flour
	½ cup hot, melted butter
Salt, pepper	Beurre Montpensier*

Empty and clean the fish, season with salt and pepper, sprinkle with flour, pour hot, melted butter over them, and set to roast in a hot oven for 10 or 12 minutes. Baste frequently.

Meanwhile, prepare the:

BEURRE MONTPENSIER

2 shallots, chopped	½ cup butter, softened
1 ounce spinach leaves	Salt, pepper
A few parsley, chervil, and fresh tarragon leaves	

Blanch the shallots and the herbs for 8 minutes. Strain and cool them and then squeeze them in a cloth to extract as much liquid as possible. Pound them in a mortar and then pass through a fine sieve. Mix the herbs into the well-softened butter and season to taste. Arrange the fish on a hot platter and serve the Beurre Montpensier separately.

One of the most fashionable and chic restaurants in Paris is *Le Berkeley*, on the Avenue Matignon, near the Rond-Point des Champs-Elysées. Here, *Monsieur Jean Rouhette*, the very able director, caters for the *élite* of international society and for well-known artists, authors, and stage and screen personalities. The restaurant is most comfortable and the service impeccable. In summer you can enjoy lunch on the flowered terrace on the sidewalk and admire the fountains and great chestnut trees on the Champs-Elysées.

The menu of Le Berkeley lists almost everything that the epicure could desire. But "Monsieur Jean," as he is known, prefers to have his meals in strict privacy, for he enjoys experimenting, with the assistance of his very experienced chef, Monsieur André Moreau, in the creation of very simple dishes from what may be left over from the preparation of *plats raffinés* for his V.I.P. clientèle. For example, for the very simple and easily prepared Poireaux au Gratin,* half the white and half the green of the leeks are used, after the lower and purely white part has been utilized for some other dish. And what could be easier to prepare than the delicious Gnocchi aux Champignons,* another of Monsieur Jean's favorite *plats simples*.

GNOCCHI AUX CHAMPIGNONS
(POTATO GNOCCHI WITH SAUTEED MUSHROOMS)

Serves 6

2 *pounds potatoes*	½ *cup butter*
1 *pound mushrooms, sliced*	*Salt, pepper*
2 *eggs*	1 *teaspoon lemon juice*
1 *cup flour*	

Peel the potatoes and cook them in boiling, salted water and proceed as if preparing a purée of potatoes. Meanwhile, wash thoroughly the mushrooms in a little water with a dash of vinegar. Dry and slice finely.

When you have mashed the cooked, dried potatoes, add the two eggs, the cup of flour, and ¼ cup softened butter, bit by bit. Season with salt and pepper and beat together thoroughly. To make gnocchis, place the dough on a wooden platter and roll it out into the form of a long, thin sausage. Cut off pieces the size of a small nut, and flatten them slightly. Then, with the aid of the prongs of a fork form gnocchis (small dumplings). Sprinkle them lightly with flour and plunge them into boiling, salted water. As soon as they rise to the surface (after 5 minutes or so), remove and strain them and place them on a hot serving dish.

Sauté the mushrooms, for 4 or 5 minutes, in the remaining ¼ cup of butter. Add the lemon juice.

Spread the cooked mushrooms evenly over the gnocchis and pour over the juice from the pan. Serve at once.

POIREAUX AU GRATIN
(LEEKS WITH SAUCE BECHAMEL AND GRATED CHEESE)

Serves 4

3 pounds leeks (half white, half green)	½ cup grated Gruyère cheese
	Bread crumbs
Salt, pepper	Butter
Sauce Béchamel*	

Plunge the thoroughly washed leeks into boiling, salted water and cook gently for about 20 minutes or until they just start to soften. Remove and drain. Butter an oval dish that will go into the oven. Salt and pepper the leeks and arrange neatly in

the dish. Pour over the Sauce Béchamel and sprinkle with
the grated cheese. Cover with bread crumbs. Dot with a few
small pieces of butter and brown under the grill.

SAUCE BECHAMEL

2 *tablespoons flour*	1½ *cups scalded milk*
2 *tablespoons butter*	*Salt, pepper*

Make a roux by mixing the flour with the melted butter in a
small pan. Stir over a low flame until it starts to color. Gradually add the milk. Continue stirring until the sauce thickens.
Salt and pepper slightly and allow to simmer for a quarter of
an hour.

Everyone who is fond of seafood knows of *La Maison Prunier*,
in the Rue Duphot, just by the Madeleine. This famous fish
restaurant is run by *Monsieur Barnagaud* whose wife, Madame Prunier, administers the London establishment in Saint
James's Street.

Fish, of course, was the main topic of conversation when
we lunched with Monsieur Barnagaud to inquire what were
his favorite simple dishes. One of them is the Mouclade
d'Esnandes,* an original way of preparing mussels with a
cream and aniseed sauce. When we discussed the art of simple cooking, we were in complete agreement concerning the
basic principles. Monsieur Barnagaud, too, we found was a
stickler for Purée de Pommes de Terre. "I will tell you exactly
how I prepare them," he told us. "And a very good accompaniment is Sautéed Kidneys."*

ROGNONS DE VEAU SAUTES, PUREE DE POMMES DE TERRE
(SAUTEED VEAL KIDNEYS WITH MASHED POTATOES)

Serves 4

4 veal kidneys
½ cup butter
2 tablespoons cognac
4 tablespoons port wine
4 tablespoons shallots, finely chopped

1 tablespoon onion, finely chopped
Parsley, finely chopped
Salt, pepper

Slice the kidneys in half lengthwise. Soak them in cold water with a dash of vinegar for 10 minutes; then remove and drain. Cut them into cubes about the size of a large lump of sugar. Sauté them rapidly, in a cocotte, in the hot butter for 1 minute. Pour in the cognac and blaze. Next add the port wine and the finely chopped shallots, the onions, and parsley. Salt and pepper. Mix well together. Cover the cocotte and cook, fairly rapidly, for 10 minutes. Remove the kidneys and keep hot. Reduce the juice in the cocotte until it starts to thicken. Rectify the seasoning and pour it over the kidneys. Serve very hot with a Purée de Pommes de Terre.*

PUREE DE POMMES DE TERRE (MASHED POTATOES)

Serves 4

2 pounds large roasting potatoes
¼ cup butter

¾ cup scalded milk
Salt, pepper

Wash the potatoes thoroughly. Do not peel them. Dry them and bake them in a hot oven for 30 minutes. When they are cooked, cut them in half, lengthwise, and remove the pulp with a spoon. Pass through a sieve and place in a warm pan, over a low flame. Add the butter bit by bit and beat well with a wooden spoon. When all the butter is absorbed, add the milk gradually, beating vigorously all the time. Season with salt and pepper and serve at once.

MOUCLADE D'ESNANDES
(MUSSELS WITH CREAM AND ANISEED SAUCE)

Serves 4

6 *pounds mussels*	2 *tablespoons flour*
1½ *cups dry white wine*	2 *cups hot milk*
Finely chopped:	18 *grains of aniseed*
2 *cloves garlic*	2 *egg yolks*
5 *shallots*	1 *tablespoon fresh cream*
1 *onion*	*Salt, pepper*
3 *tablespoons butter*	

Scrape and brush the mussels well in several waters. Place them in a large pan, add the white wine, cover securely, and cook rapidly for 5 or 6 minutes, shaking the pan vigorously several times during the cooking process.

Remove the mussels and keep hot. Strain the juice from the pan through a cheesecloth and reserve.

Cook the garlic, the shallots, and the onion in the butter, very gently for about 30 minutes, in a small pan with a very closely fitting lid. The vegetables should soften and not color. Next add the flour and mix thoroughly to make a roux. Then add the juice in which the mussels have cooked and, gradually, the hot milk. Stir well and add the aniseed and leave the sauce to simmer for 20 minutes.

In the meantime, remove the upper shell from the mussels and place the mussels in their half shells on the bottom of four hot plates. Remove the sauce from the fire and beat in the egg yolks and the cream. Rectify the seasoning. Pour the sauce over the plates of mussels and serve at once.

More Recipes
from the Paris Bistros

Of the thirty recipes given here, seventeen originate from bistros the names and addresses of which appeared in *Paris Bistro Cookery* (published in London, in 1957, by MacGibbon & Kee; in New York, in 1958, by Alfred Knopf; in Zürich, in 1958, by Rascher Verlag; and in Bussum, Holland, in 1959, by G. J. A. Ruys).

These new recipes, from some of our favorite old haunts in the bistro world of Paris, comprise several worthwhile and interesting discoveries, such as the extremely simple Croque Moujic Russe* (Chez Georges), the clever combination of the Beurre d'Escargots with the Coquilles Saint-Jacques* (Le Grand Comptoir), the incomparable Rognons Flambés* (Le Ruban Bleu), and the intriguing Irish Stew à la Provençale* (Chez Quinson).

The other thirteen recipes have been kindly supplied by the proprietor-chefs of eight newly discovered bistros. Those in possession of *Paris Bistro Cookery* may care to append details of them to the book, by way of bringing the list of recommended Paris bistros up to date. As for these recipes, many a housewife may now discover that it is not nearly so difficult as thought to prepare a Terrine de Foies de Volaille Truffée* (Au Bocage Fleuri). As far as easy vegetable dishes are concerned, I recommend highly the Ratatouille* (Aux Charpentiers). We have tried this out several times in our own kitchen and have slightly altered the quantities of some of the ingredients to suit our own taste, which brings me back to what I have mentioned in the Culinary Introduction, about exactness in cooking being difficult to achieve.

PART ONE

Soups:

Minestrone au Riz (serves 4).

Entrées:

Terrine de Foies de Volaille Truffée (serves 15).

Fowl:

Poularde Marie-Louise (serves 6).
Poulet au Blanc, Pommes Dauphine (serves 4).
Poulet Sauté à l'Estragon (serves 4).

Meat:

Boeuf Saignant à la Ficelle (serves 6).
Blanquette de Veau (serves 4).
Steak au Poivre Albert (serves 4).
Rognons Turbigo (serves 4).

Vegetable Dishes:

Pommes Dauphine (serves 4).
Ratatouille (serves 4).
Risi-Bisi (serves 6).

Salads:

Salade Niçoise (serves 4).

PART TWO

Soups:

Soupe Normande (serves 4).
Crème Valdèze (serves 4).

Entrées:

Jambon Florentine au Gratin (serves 4).
Croque Moujic Russe (serves 4).

Fish:

Homard Grillé à la Diable (serves 2).
Coquille Saint-Jacques, Beurre d'Escargot (serves 3).

Fowl:
>Canard aux Pêches (serves 4).

Rabbit:
>Rable de Lapin à la Moutarde (serves 4).

Meat:
>Rognons Pamplona (serves 4).
>Irish Stew à la Provençale (serves 6).
>La Potée (serves 8 to 10).
>Rôti de Veau Thermidor (serves 8 to 10).
>Rognons Flambés Ruban Bleu (serves 4).
>Côtes de Mouton Champvallon (serves 4).
>Rognons à la Moutarde (serves 4).
>Steak au Beurre d'Echalotes avec Gratin Dauphinois (serves 4).

Vegetable Dishes:
>Gratin Dauphinois (serves 4).
>Epinards à la Crème (serves 4).

PART ONE

CHEZ MARIE-LOUISE
52, Rue Championnet
Paris, 18ème. Tel. Montmartre 86–55
Closed Sunday evenings and Mondays;
also during August

Three years ago I discovered a tiny bistro way up in Montmartre called *Le Saint-Pierre*. The name of *la patronne* was *Marie-Louise* and it was she who did all the cooking which was excellent. But the next time I called there I found that she and her husband had moved to a small restaurant of their own in the neighborhood, called *Chez Marie-Louise*. This is in a rather lost district of Paris but a most useful address to know for those who may be visiting the nearby Marché aux Puces. When I returned recently to enjoy some of Marie-

Louise's specialties, I found that she was no longer there: she had retired.

This is the way it often goes with the bistros in Paris and one has to keep continual track of them or, rather, of their proprietors. But once a bistro proprietor has earned a reputation for the constant good quality of his wine and food then he may be sure that his clientèle will remain faithful to him and follow him wherever he may reopen in the city, as in the case, for example, of *Monsieur Moissonnier* who has recently reopened his bistro opposite the main entrance to the Halles aux Vins.

I was given a warm welcome Chez Marie-Louise by the new chef-proprietor, *Monsieur Coillot*, who has attempted to make little alteration in the restaurant, its interior, and its cuisine. Monsieur Coillot is an experienced chef; the last place he was working at was the Lapérouse (three-star) Restaurant on the Quai des Grands-Augustins. Monsieur Coillot is from Burgundy and his very attractive wife, who serves in the restaurant, is from the Allier.

Chez Marie-Louise is small, quiet, unassuming. There are seven tables on the ground floor and eight on the first floor. It is pleasantly decorated: copper pans hanging on the walls, green tablecloths, and a bouquet of flowers always standing by the neat little bar.

With very few changes, Monsieur Coillot has retained Marie-Louise's menu card. The specialties remain as before: Lotte Maçonnaise, Filets de Saint-Pierre, Boeuf Saignant à la Ficelle,* and the famous Poularde Marie-Louise.* One of Monsieur's Coillot's most successful additions to the menu is his Entrecôte "Marchand de Vin."

Monsieur Coillot's list of *vins de provenance directe* is a standard one of the better quality wines. I recommend the Pouilly Fuissé and the Pouilly Fumé among the whites; the Côtes de Provence and the Rosé de Sancerre among the pinks; and the Chiroubles and Saint-Amour among the reds. I also recommend either the Marc de Bourgogne or the Eau-de-Vie de Poire William with your coffee. Prices are very reasonable.

POULARDE MARIE-LOUISE
(CHICKEN MARIE-LOUISE)

Serves 6

1 *large frying chicken*	¾ *bottle dry white wine*
⅓ *cup butter*	2 *cloves garlic*
2 *tablespoons cognac*	2 *tablespoons flour*
½ *cup onions, chopped*	*Salt, pepper*
2 *pounds tomatoes, peeled,*	½ *tablespoon French mustard*
seeded, and quartered	¼ *cup fresh cream*

Cut up the chicken. Brown the pieces slightly on all sides, in the butter, in a casserole, for about 10 minutes. Pour over the cognac—which should be slightly warmed—and blaze. Remove the pieces of chicken and keep hot. Add the onions to the casserole and cook till soft, then add the tomatoes. Cook for 10 minutes, then pour in the white wine and bring gently back to the boil. Add the garlic.

Remove the casserole from the fire. Make a thin paste of the flour mixed with a little of the liquid from the casserole. Pour slowly into the casserole, stirring all the time. Replace the chicken. Salt and pepper. Mix well together all the ingredients in the casserole, cover, and cook gently for about half an hour, or until the pieces of chicken are tender.

Remove the chicken and keep hot. Reduce the sauce in the casserole by almost half, then strain it through a fine sieve, having removed the 2 cloves of garlic. Pour the sauce back into the casserole and mix in the mustard. When the sauce has almost reached the boiling point again, remove from the fire and add, carefully, the cream, stirring with a wooden spoon, *being careful that the sauce does not boil again, otherwise it will turn, as there is also flour among the ingredients.* Pour the sauce over the pieces of chicken and serve at once.

BOEUF SAIGNANT A LA FICELLE
(RUMP OF BEEF COOKED IN A VEGETABLE BROTH)

Serves 6

*Pot-au-Feu**   *2 pounds beef, cut from the rump*

Prepare the Pot-au-Feu as indicated but without the shin of beef. Boil, with all the vegetables, for 1 hour, then drop the piece of beef into the pot, having tied it up with a butcher's string and leaving a length of it hanging outside the pot. Boil rapidly for 5 minutes, then reduce the heat to cook gently for about 30 minutes. Then pull out the meat with the aid of the string. It will be tender, slightly underdone, and imbued with the flavor of the vegetables and the herbs. You can judge the state of doneness of the meat by pressing it with the fingers. If you think it is too "rare" for your taste, then replace for a few more minutes in the pot.

Serve the meat, sliced, in the middle of a large, hot serving dish with the vegetables from the pot, in addition to small new potatoes and French Beans,* arranged neatly all around.

AU BOCAGE FLEURI
19, Rue Duranton
Paris, 15ème. Tel. Vaugirard 43–17
Closed Sundays and Mondays and during August

There is much to be said in praise of this charming little restaurant which is located in a lost quarter of Paris. As far as tourists are concerned there is absolutely nothing of interest to be seen in this district. But many are the foreign gastronomes "in the know" who come this far from the center of the city to enjoy Monsieur Bak's exceptional *cuisine*.

Admittedly, Au Bocage Fleuri is not a bistro of the rough-and-ready type. But I like to think of it in terms of a bistro as Monsieur Bak, the proprietor, does all the cooking, while his wife and one waitress serve at table. Thus, the atmosphere is *intime* and friendly. The interior is cosy and comfortable and is gaily decorated in the fashion of a Normandy inn.

Monsieur Bak, who comes from Normandy, makes a specialty of Grenouilles and Coquilles Saint-Jacques; a magnificent (and not overrich) Terrine de Foies de Volailles Truffée*; and, of course, the three great Normandy specialties, Sole Normande, Ris de Veau Normand, and Poulet de Bresse Vallée d'Auge. In my opinion there is no other restaurateur who can surpass Monsieur Bak in the preparation of his Poulet Vallée d'Auge. It is superb. Among the desserts I recommend the Pêche Cardinal and the Soufflée Grand Marnier.

The wines to drink are the Sancerre, the Muscadet, and the Zwicker (a delightful, light, dry Alsatian wine) among the whites; and the Fleurie as the red wine. Don't fail to taste the wonderful old Calvados with your coffee.

Charges Au Bocage Fleuri are reasonable for a comfortable little restaurant of this category.

TERRINE DE FOIES DE VOLAILLE TRUFFEE
(TERRINE OF CHICKEN LIVERS AND TRUFFLES)

Approximately 15 slices

Most recipes for terrines and pâtés are complicated and take a long time to prepare. But this is certainly not the case with this terrine which is one of Monsieur Bak's specialties.

1½ *pounds chicken livers*	*Salt, pepper*
Equal quantities:	3 *medium-sized onions, finely*
Dry white wine	*chopped*
Cognac	2 *cloves garlic, finely chopped*
2 *pounds lower neck of pork,*	3 *truffles*
finely chopped	2 *eggs, beaten*
2 *pounds breast (hand) of*	1 *tablespoon flour*
pork, finely chopped	3 *broad strips of larding pork*
	Bouquet garni

Place the chicken livers in a bowl and pour in sufficient equal quantities of dry white wine and cognac just to cover them. Leave to marinate for 24 hours.

Remove four of the chicken livers and reserve them for later use. Chop up the rest of the chicken livers very finely along with the neck and the breast (hand) of pork. Season with salt and pepper. Add the onions, the garlic, and 2 of the 3 truffles also finely chopped. Mix well together with 2 tablespoons of cognac, the 2 beaten eggs and the flour.

Line the terrine with the larding pork and place the mixture inside. In the center, arrange the remaining four whole chicken livers and the remaining truffle, sliced. On top, place the bouquet garni. Cover the terrine with the lid (which should have an escape hole) and cook in a hot oven for about 3 hours, after which time remove. Take out the bouquet garni and place a weight of approximately 3 pounds on a dish on top of the uncovered terrine. Leave to cool and compress for 5 or 6 hours. Remove the weight, replace the lid of the terrine and leave to chill in the refrigerator.

LE PETIT CLOS
62, Rue de Babylone and 37 Rue Barbet-de-Jouy
Paris, 7ème. Tel. Invalides 47–73
Closed Sundays and during August

And it *is* small, this little "enclosure" of a restaurant at the corner of the rues Babylone and Barbet-de-Jouy. There are seven tables only and almost half of this tiny restaurant is devoted to the neat, very comfortable little bar which you find on your left as you enter. Here Monsieur and Madame Bernheim will greet you and serve you an apéritif while you await your table, but I strongly recommend that you telephone and make a reservation, for this miniature restaurant is the only one of its kind in this quarter which is crowded with ministries and town houses.

I must admit that this is hardly a bistro in the strict sense of the word but I am including it here as the atmosphere is that of a *sympathique* bistro with *le patron* and *la patronne* waiting on you.

Apart from ministers and their minions from around the corner, Le Petit Clos is also frequented by a discerning clientèle among whom are several of the well-known titled residents—dukes and countesses galore—in the adjacent Rue Barbet-de-Jouy who appreciate the fine wine and food that is served here in a friendly, unpretentious, and relaxing atmosphere.

Le Petit Clos was formerly owned by Le Comte de Chavagnac, a direct descendant of Lafayette, hence the reason why it is likewise frequented by both American and British tourists. Monsieur Bernheim has made few changes in the restaurant since he took over a few months ago. The décor remains much the same, the waiters are still there and the service is very attentive.

What is most interesting is that the chef at Le Petit Clos,

Monsieur Georges Dubost, has had the rare distinction of working under Alexandre Dumaine, the greatest living chef in France, to whom this book is dedicated. Monsieur Dubost's specialties are Foie-Gras à l'Armagnac, Jambon de Savoie Fumé à la Cheminée, Croutes au Fromage, Le Lapin Clos (rabbit served with a delicious French mustard and cream sauce), Cous-Cous (served on Thursdays), Pot-au-Feu à la Moelle (served on Saturdays in winter), Poulet au Blanc,* and l'Omelette Fourée aux Framboises. Now another new recipe has been added to this intriguing menu. It is the sensational Crêpes de Sole Petit Clos (fillets of sole with a mushroom and cream sauce wrapped and cooked in pancakes).

Another specialty at Le Petit Clos is the Fondue Bourguignonne. To the best of my knowledge and belief this is the only restaurant in Paris where this original dish is served. What makes La Fondue Bourguignonne fascinating is the cook-it-yourself idea of the dish. Each person is supplied with a bib and a long bone-handled fork with which to cook the cubes of sirloin steak in a mixture of boiling oil and butter which bubbles in a small enameled steel pot set atop a burner placed in the middle of your table. You spear the meat and hold it in the pot until cooked to your own desired state of doneness. You then place the pieces of meat on your hot plate —you must be very careful not to pop the meat straight into your mouth from the burning cooking fork—and consume them with one of the three sauces, curry, ketchup, *aioli* (garlic), or a mixture of chopped gherkins, raw onions, and parsley which are neatly arranged around the cubes of raw meat set in the center of the serving dish.

With this gay and entertaining dish—such a pleasant change from the humdrum dishes à la carte—you have some excellent vintage Bordeaux and Burgundies to choose from the wine list, which also includes an authentic Muscadet to drink with the hors d'oeuvre and the entrées, and a Brouilly to accompany the meat and fowl dishes. You should taste the exceptional Eau-de-Vie de Poire with your coffee.

POULET AU BLANC, POMMES DAUPHINE

Serves 4

A tender chicken of 2½ pounds	2 egg yolks
½ pound butter	Salt, pepper

Cut the chicken up into four pieces and sauté gently in a casserole in the butter. Be careful that the chicken does not color as the meat must remain white (hence the name for this dish). Salt and pepper and close the casserole hermetically and cook gently for three quarters of an hour. Remove the quartered chicken and keep hot.

Beat the egg yolks in a little water. Remove the casserole from the fire and mix in the butter with the juice from the chicken. Pour the sauce over the quartered chicken and serve at once with . . .

POMMES DAUPHINE

. . . which are made by mixing one part of Pâte à Chou with three parts Mashed Potatoes*:

PATE A CHOU
(CREAM PUFF PASTE)

½ cup hot water	2 eggs
½ cup flour	Pinch of salt
¼ cup butter	

Melt the butter in a small casserole. Pour in the hot water and add the pinch of salt and bring gently to a boil. Add the flour and stir vigorously over a low flame until the mixture leaves the sides of the pan and forms a ball in the center. Remove the casserole from the fire and incorporate the eggs one at a time. Beat thoroughly until the batter thickens.

Add this Pâte à Chou to the dried Mashed Potatoes and leave to cool. Make Pommes Dauphine by shaping the mixture into balls the size of golf balls. Roll them in flour and fry them in hot fat until they are puffed and golden brown. Drain on absorbent paper and serve very hot along with the chicken.

AUX CHARPENTIERS
10, Rue Mabillon
Paris, 6ème. Tel. Danton 30–05
Closed Saturday and Sunday and during August

This is a real honest-to-God bistro where the atmosphere is
friendly and the comfort adequate. Here you will find *le zinc*
to the left as you enter, sawdust on the floor, paper tablecloths, the inaccessible peg for your coat and hat, the pigeon-
hole rack for the napkins of the regular customers, and the
upright basket for the "bastards," the long French loaves of
bread.

Aux Charpentiers is located in a quiet, narrow little street
that runs alongside the Marché Saint-Germain, a fascinating
market on the left bank where I myself do most of my shopping. It is close to Saint-Germain-des-Près with its collec-
tion of famous cafés, Les Deux Magots, Le Flore, and Brasse-
rie Lipp, meeting places of the theatrical crowd, the
littérateurs, and well-known artists; as well as phoney poets
and painters. This is an ideal bistro to dine at before sipping
your coffee on the terrace of one of these cafés and watching
this strange world go by.

Aux Charpentiers got its name from the fact that this bistro
was the rendezvous, in the early thirties, of the carpenters of
the quarter, who used to come, and sometimes still do come,
to enjoy a hearty and cheap meal.

Le patron is Monsieur Puyalon (otherwise known as
Charles) who surveys the simple, but very good bourgeois,
cooking in the kitchen. His wife, Maria, makes all the cakes
and pastries, for which the bistro is famous, such as the impos-
ing Gâteau Napoleon.

Spécialités de la maison are the Ratatouille,* the Timbale
de Homard et Langouste Shanghai, grilled meats, and the
Filets de Caneton, Sauce aux Olives. Prices are in the def-

initely cheap category. The white wines to drink are the Aligoté and the Sylvaner; the reds, the Beaujolais and the Côte du Rhône.

RATATOUILLE
(VEGETABLE CASSEROLE PROVENCALE)

Serves 4

This easily prepared vegetable dish originates from the shores of the Mediterranean. It can be eaten hot or cold. It can also be used as a filling for an omelette.

2½ cups zucchini (vegetable marrow), peeled and sliced
¾ cup onions, chopped
1 cup sweet green pepper, chopped
3 tablespoons olive oil
2½ cups aubergines (eggplant), sliced

2½ cups tomatoes, peeled, seeded, and quartered
1 tablespoon tomato purée
Salt, pepper
Fresh tarragon
2 cloves garlic, finely chopped
1 tablespoon of parsley, chopped

Cook the vegetable marrow, the onions, and the sweet peppers in the oil for 5 or 6 minutes. Slice or quarter, but do not peel, the well-washed aubergines. Add to the pan along with the tomatoes. Season with salt and pepper, add a little fresh chopped tarragon, cover, and cook gently until the mixture is well blended and just starts to soften. Add the garlic and the parsley and cook for another 15 minutes, or until the liquid in the pan starts to disappear and the sauce thickens.

CHEZ RENE
12, Boulevard Saint-Germain
Paris, 5ème. Tel. Odeon 30–23
Closed Mondays and during August

Chez René is one of my favorite Paris bistros. René himself used to manage the popular and crowded bistro, Le Beaujolais, on the Quai de la Tournelle. Then, about four years ago, he opened his own bistro just around the corner, on the Boulevard Saint-Germain. Chez René is the ideal place for you to go and have lunch after wandering around the Ile Saint-Louis and visiting the historic mansions on the island, the Hôtel de Lauzun and the Hôtel Lambert.

René's little bistro is very neat and tidy. Apart from the rows of salami sausages hanging from the ceiling, there is little décor; it is the wine and food that count. You sit on comfortable red banquettes at bakelite tables covered with paper tablecloths. You will be greeted by René himself as soon as you enter and he will offer you a glass of vin blanc cassis (dry white wine with black currant juice) at the bar before you sit down at table which, it is imperative, you should have reserved beforehand.

Here, in René's small, animated, tightly packed bistro, a faithful clientèle of exacting French gourmets come to enjoy Madame René's specialties from the Mâconnais and Beaujolais regions, among which I recommend the Quenelles de Brochet à la Crème and the Coq au Vin; not to mention the grilled meats.

There is a fixed *plat du jour* for every day of the week, except Mondays when the restaurant is closed. Thus, you are enabled to decide, according to your gastronomic preference, when to lunch, or dine, Chez René. On Tuesday, Haricot de Mouton is served. On Wednesday, it is Boeuf Bourguignon. On Thursday, Boeuf à la Mode. On Friday, Blanquette de Veau.* On Saturday, Boeuf Gros Sel. And on Sunday, Gigot de Mouton. Prices are very reasonable.

The Beaujolais wines, which René has sent direct from the vineyards and which he bottles himself, are of truly exceptional quality and are also very reasonable in price. René himself comes from Julienas, in the heart of the Beaujolais country, which explains the regular attendance of wine connoisseurs at his bistro.

BLANQUETTE DE VEAU
(BLANQUETTE OF VEAL)

Serves 4

There are different ways of making this classic dish. I, myself, always refer to Madame René's recipe as I find it the easiest and one that never fails.

2 *pounds shoulder of veal*	*Salt, pepper*
⅓ *cup butter*	*Warm water*
8 *small onions*	½ *pound mushrooms, sliced*
4 *tablespoons flour*	1 *egg yolk*
½ *cup dry white wine*	1 *teaspoon lemon juice*
Bouquet garni	1 *cup fresh cream*
2 *carrots, sliced*	

Cut the veal into 1½-inch cubes and brown them in the butter, in a casserole. Add the onions and also brown them slightly. Add the flour to make a roux, then pour in the white wine. Add the bouquet garni, carrots, salt and pepper. Pour in sufficient warm water to come to the surface of the meat. Cover and simmer for one and a half hours. A quarter of an hour before removing the casserole, add the sliced mushrooms.

Whisk the egg yolk in the lemon juice. Remove the casserole from the fire and slowly add the egg and lemon juice to the Blanquette, stirring all the time. Pour in the cream and mix well. Keep hot, but be careful not to let it boil, otherwise the sauce will turn. Serve at once with rice.

CHEZ ALBERT
122, Avenue du Maine
Paris, 14ème. Tel. Suffren 47–62
Closed Mondays and during August

Albert's trim little bistro type of restaurant in the Avenue du Maine, over in the fourteenth arrondissement, is an address well worth noting for it is the only place of its kind in this distant quarter of Paris. If you are interested in painting then you should lunch, or dine, Chez Albert, for here you will be served fine quality food and wine and, maybe, have the chance of sitting next to some of the better known of the younger generation of the artists of the School of Paris, such as Carzou and Clavé, both of whom live nearby.

Albert comes from Normandy, his wife from Burgundy. So it is only natural to expect that the food that comes out of their kitchen should be something out of the ordinary as, indeed, it is. There is always plenty to choose from on the menu card. Apart from a very substantial *plat du jour*, the *spécialités de la maison* are Terrine de Canard du Chef, Terrine de Foies de Volaille,* Truite aux Amandes, Cuisses de Grenouilles Sautées Provençales, Steak au Poivre,* Coq au Vin, Poulet Sauté à l'Estragon.* In addition, there is an appetizing selection of grilled meats.

For a restaurant of this size there is a remarkable range of wines to accompany these dishes. If you are a real connoisseur, Albert can produce something exceptional for you in the way of vintage Burgundy or Bordeaux. Otherwise, there is an excellent choice of regional wines: Quincy, Muscadet, Chavignol, among the whites; and Brouilly, Chiroubles, Côtes du Rhône, among the reds.

It is very pleasant, in summertime, to be able to sit out-of-doors Chez Albert and enjoy a quiet lunch on the flowered terrace on the sidewalk. The restaurant inside is cosily furnished, with bouquets of flowers and several paintings by young artists hanging on the walls.

Albert, who surveys the cooking in the kitchen, has a very capable chef working for him. He has spent some time in Canada and in America, so if you feel like tasting something that will remind you of home, you can, perhaps, persuade Albert to have it prepared for you.

Charges at Chez Albert are reasonable.

It is advisable to telephone and book your table as the restaurant is always full, the reason being that many a faithful client of Albert—when he was director of the well-known Dagorno Restaurant, opposite the Villette slaughter-house—has followed him to this new and fashionable little restaurant of his own in the Avenue du Maine.

POULET SAUTE A L'ESTRAGON
(FRIED CHICKEN WITH TARRAGON)

Serves 4

1 *tender frying chicken*	*Bouquet garni:*
Salt, pepper	1 *bay leaf*
2 *tablespoons flour*	*Sprig thyme*
¼ *cup butter*	*Sprig parsley*
2 *shallots, chopped*	1 *branch fresh tarragon*
½ *cup dry white wine*	*Chicken bouillon (or water)*
1 *tablespoon tomato purée*	*Croutons*

Cut the chicken into four pieces. Salt and pepper them and dredge them in flour. Melt the butter in a stewpan and brown the pieces of chicken lightly on all sides. Add the shallots and sprinkle the pieces of chicken with the remaining flour, and turn several times so as to absorb all the flour into the juice in the pan.

Add the white wine and the tomato purée and the bouquet garni and pour in sufficient bouillon (or water) to cover the pieces of chicken. Stir well and simmer for about 20 minutes then add most of the fresh chopped tarragon. Leave to simmer for about another 10 minutes.

Remove the pieces of chicken and arrange them on a hot serving dish, with croutons around. Pour the sauce over the chicken and sprinkle with what is left of the chopped tarragon. Serve with new potatoes and French Beans.*

STEAK AU POIVRE ALBERT
(PEPPER STEAK)

Serves 4

4 *small, unsweetened pancakes*	3 *tablespoons butter*
Coarsely ground black pepper	2 *tablespoons oil*
	¼ *cup dry white wine*
4 *sirloin steaks*	2 *tablespoons cognac*
Salt	½ *cup fresh cream*

Make four plain, unsweetened pancakes. Keep warm.

Press plenty of coarsely ground black pepper into both sides of the steak. Sprinkle lightly with salt. Heat the butter and the oil in a frying pan and sear the steaks quickly on either side over a fast flame. Lower the heat and cook as required (preferably "rare"). Remove the steaks and keep hot on a serving dish that will go into the oven.

Discard the juice in the frying pan and pour in the white wine. Add the cognac and the cream. Allow the sauce to reduce gently, stirring all the time, by about one third; or until it starts to thicken. Place a folded pancake partly over each one of the steaks. Pour over the sauce and heat under the hot grill until they start to brown. Remove and serve at once with straw potatoes or Pommes Pont-Neuf.*

UNSWEETENED PANCAKES

(This is calculated for *twelve* portions: from a practical point of view it is a waste of time to prepare only *four* pancakes.)

Anyway, if there are ten or twelve for lunch or dinner, then all you have to do is to adjust the proportions of the other ingredients for making these Steaks au Poivre Albert accordingly.

¾ *cup flour*	2 *tablespoons oil*
Pinch of salt	1½ *cups milk*
2 *eggs*	1½ *tablespoons melted* (*nut*
1 *egg yolk*	*brown*) *butter*

Place all the ingredients in a bowl and beat together to obtain a smooth and not too thick batter. Cook the pancakes, as for Crèpes Suzette, in a hot, slightly oiled frying pan.

AUBERGE NOTRE-DAME
65, Quai de la Tournelle
Paris, 5ème. Tel. Danton 52–69
Closed Sundays in summer and during latter half of August

After a tiring tour sightseeing on the Ile de la Cité (La Conciergerie, La Sainte-Chapelle, Notre-Dame) go and relax and enjoy the comfort and the excellent wine and food that are served at the Auberge Notre-Dame, a relatively new, chic little restaurant which is much *en vogue.* Dominique and Janine, the owners, who help serve in the restaurant, cater to a discerning clientèle of Parisian and foreign gourmets who, if I am not mistaken, are keeping quiet their "discovery" of this entertaining little restaurant.

The interior decoration of the Auberge is amusing and original. A wooden banquette with comfortable, brightly colored cushions, wooden tables, and wooden chairs are ranged along one side of the narrow little room, the wall of which is decorated with multicolored little bowls and saucers, in which V.I.P.s visiting the restaurant are requested to sign their names in red paint. An original way of keeping a Livre d'Or!

On the opposite side of the room is an attractive bar *à l'espagnole,* built of white stone and wood. There is soft, indirect lighting and, in the evenings, there are long tapering candles flickering on the tables which cast a warm glow on the straw mats and the gay little napkins. There are twelve tables in all, four of which are on the enclosed terrace from where you get an impressive view of Notre-Dame, especially at night when the great cathedral is floodlit.

The cuisine at the Auberge Notre-Dame, prepared by the chef, Monsieur Robert, is Franco-Spanish. There is a different *plat du jour* for every day of the week, except for Sundays when the restaurant is closed. This might be a Poulet Grillé American, Petit Salé aux Lentilles, Potée aux Choux, Piccata, Paella à la Valencienne, or a Puchero, which is a sensational Spanish Pot-au-Feu consisting of pork, beef, chicken, stuffed sausage, potatoes, cabbage, and chick peas.

Everyday specialties of the Auberge are the Terrine du Chef (made of duck, goose, and rabbit), Assiette de Cochon-ailles (an endless selection of pâtés and sausages that are de-livered regularly to the restaurant from different regions of France and which are served with various kinds of country bread). Coquelet à la Broche aux Aromates, and Côte de Boeuf Grillée à la Moelle. There is also a carefully prepared Salade Niçoise* with a special sauce, for which I give the recipe here.

There is a good selection of vintage wines to choose from. Among the regional wines, I recommend the dry, white Pouilly-Fuissé and the Maçon Blanc; and the Beaujolais to accompany the grilled meats.

You must telephone and reserve your table, otherwise you will never get into the Auberge Notre-Dame.

SALADE NICOISE

Serves 4

This is the classic way of making a Salade Niçoise. Monsieur Dominique, however, leaves out the garlic and the chopped onions among the ingredients for, as he rightly points out, they are not to everybody's taste. They can be added, or left out, as you wish.

Garlic, optional
1 *tablespoon chopped onions, optional*
1 *large heart of lettuce, cut in broad strips; or, leaves of endives, halved*
1 *sweet green pepper, cut in rings*
12 *black olives*

½ *cup cooked French beans*
1 *can tuna fish*
2 *hard-boiled eggs, halved*
4 *tomatoes, quartered*
8 *fillets anchovies*
2 *tablespoons finely chopped fresh tarragon, chervil, and parsley (1 tablespoon for the sauce)*

If you are using the garlic, then rub a large salad bowl (preferably a wooden one) with a clove of garlic. Place in the ingredients, arranging neatly on top the tuna fish, the halved eggs, the quartered tomatoes, and the anchovies. Sprinkle with one tablespoon of the chopped mixed herbs. Place in the refrigerator until required.

Serve first the eggs, the tuna fish, and the anchovies. Then pour over the sauce. Turn the salad well several times before serving.

You can vary the ingredients according to your own taste and add, for example, cold, sliced, cooked potatoes; cucumber; celery; raw cauliflower; radishes; etc.

SAUCE DOMINIQUE

4 *fillets of anchovies*
1 *tablespoon mixed herbs (see above)*
½ *hard-boiled egg*

4 *tablespoons olive oil*
½ *tablespoon wine vinegar*
Salt, pepper

Pound together thoroughly the anchovies, herbs and the half egg. Add to the mixed olive oil and the vinegar. Add a little freshly ground pepper. Salt should not be necessary, on account of the anchovies.

AUBERGE DES DOLOMITES
38, Rue Poncelet
Paris, 17ème. Tel. Carnot 94–56
Closed during August

There exist a considerable number of Italian restaurants in Paris, many of them excellent, but one which, I think, is unique in its own way, is l'Auberge des Dolomites. For the very able proprietor, Signor Vitti, has had the foresight to offer his Parisian, Italian, and foreign clientèle a continual selection of Italian regional specialties. A French restaurant abroad usually serves the standard dishes of France; just as Italian restaurateurs serve their own national dishes in other countries. But, in this respect, Signor Vitti differs, for here, in Paris, he specializes in the dishes of northern Italy, and there are many of them, such as Scampi Grillés Comme à Venise, Escalope Farcie à la Bolognese and, when in season, Civet de Lièvre à la Grappa avec Polenta (served on Wednesdays), and Bolliti Misti (served on Saturdays). This last-named dish is a staggering display of *viandes et volailles gros sel*.

Signor Vitti opened his comfortable, very well serviced little Auberge des Dolomites, situated in a quiet street off the Place des Ternes, near the Etoile, five years ago, since when he has done non-stop business. Apart from the quality of the food served (and the specialty of the delicious, light Vin des Dolomites) it is, of course, the careful and expert preparation of the dishes that contribute so much to the success of the attractive and *intime* Auberge des Dolomites. The chef is Signor Gianni Filiberti, who was formerly in charge of the kitchens of the Gritti Palace Hotel in Venice; which explains much.

The Italian hors d'oeuvre, especially those served in summer, are sensational. Here you will have presented to you a tantalizing assortment of dishes such as Courgettes à la

Milanaise aux Amandes, Courgettes au Basilic, Piments farcis, Aubergines farcies, Tomates au Riz à la Romaine, Fonds d'Artichauts à la Juive, Petits Oignons confits aux Raisins Secs, Salade Espagnole, etc., along with innumerable *charcuteries italiennes* and a huge bouquet of *crudités!*

Charges are reasonable. To complete a very satisfactory meal, I recommend the very delicate Zabaione au Marsala.

RISI-BISI
(VENETIAN RISOTTO WITH PEAS)

Serves 6

⅓ *cup onions, finely chopped*
2 *tablespoons butter*
2 *cups long-grain rice*
1 *tablespoon dry white wine, warmed (optional)*

4 *cups boiling consommé (or water)*
1½ *cups cooked peas*
1½ *cups chopped ham*
¾ *cup grated Parmesan cheese*
Salt, pepper

Soften the onions in one tablespoon of butter in the bottom of a medium-sized copper casserole. When they start to color, add the dry, unwashed rice and mix well together with a wooden spoon, over a medium flame for about one minute only. Pour in the warmed white wine and the boiling consommé, or water. Cover the casserole with a folded, clean dishcloth, and on top place four plates. Simmer for 20 to 25 minutes, by which time the liquid should have evaporated and the rice should be perfectly cooked. If the rice is still somewhat soggy, then cook for another 5 minutes or so.

Remove the casserole from the fire and add the hot cooked peas and the chopped ham. Next, add the grated cheese, salt and pepper, and then the remaining tablespoon of butter (which should be softened). Mix well all together carefully and slowly. Place in a preheated mold. Cover with a large serving plate, turn upside down and serve at once.

ROGNONS TURBIGO
(VEAL KIDNEYS TURBIGO)

Serves 4

2 *veal kidneys, each weighing*	4 *hearts of artichokes*
½ *pound*	8 *medium-sized mushroom*
Salt, pepper	*caps*
Flour	4 *chipolata (pork) sausages*
4 *tablespoons butter*	5 *medium-sized firm tomatoes*
Olive oil	¼ *cup Madeira*
2 *croutons, for the kidneys*	*Beurre manié*

Soak the kidneys in cold water with a dash of vinegar for ten minutes, then remove and drain on absorbent paper. Salt and pepper them, and then roll them in a little flour. Heat the butter in a deep frying pan, add a teaspoon of olive oil and brown the kidneys on all sides, over a medium flame, for 15 minutes. Meanwhile, prepare two croutons by cutting slices of bread the same size as the kidneys and frying them lightly, till golden brown, in butter. Remove the kidneys from the pan, place them on the croutons, and keep hot.

Poach the hearts of artichokes and the mushrooms in acidulated water. The mushrooms will require about 10 minutes to cook; the hearts of artichokes about half an hour. Grill the chipolatas and four of the tomatoes.

While these vegetables are cooking, prepare the sauce by adding the Madeira to the pan in which the kidneys have been browned. Stir well and, after 5 minutes, incorporate the beurre manié (one ounce butter mixed with half a tablespoon flour) piece by piece. Reduce the sauce carefully by half. Peel, seed, and dice the fifth tomato and add to the sauce along with a walnut-size piece of butter. Simmer the sauce for another 5 or 6 minutes, stirring with a wooden spoon.

Arrange the kidneys on the croutons in the middle of a very hot serving dish and place the chipolatas and the vegetables around them. Pour over the sauce from the pan, bring to the table, halve each of the kidneys and serve at once.

MINESTRONE AU RIZ
(ITALIAN VEGETABLE SOUP WITH RICE)

Serves 4

½ medium-sized onion, finely chopped

2 tablespoons oil

½ cup butter

½ cup carrots, diced

½ cup turnips, diced

¾ cup potatoes, diced

¼ cup vegetable marrow, diced

¼ cup celery, diced

¼ cup leeks, diced

¼ cup fresh peas

¾ cup white cabbage, cut in strips

4 pints bouillon (or water)

½ cup rice

Salt, pepper

Seasoning

Grated Parmesan cheese

SEASONING

Finely chop:

2 tablespoons fat bacon

4 sprigs parsley

2 sprigs rosemary

2 leaves sage

1 small clove garlic

1 walnut-size piece of butter

Soften the finely chopped onion in the oil and butter in a pot, preferably an earthenware one for making soups. Add the diced vegetables, with the exception of the cabbage which should be cooked separately in boiling, salted water. Braise the vegetables gently for 10 to 15 minutes then add the bouillon (or water). Cover and simmer until the vegetables are almost cooked, then add the cabbage and the rice, salt and pepper slightly, and simmer for another 15 minutes.

Meanwhile prepare the seasoning by mixing well all the ingredients into a paste which should be incorporated into the soup a few minutes before removing the pot from the fire. Serve the grated Parmesan cheese separately.

PART TWO

LE CATALAN
16, Rue des Grand-Augustins
Paris, 6ème. Tel. Danton 46–07
Open for dinner only
Closed Sundays and during August

In *Paris Cuisine* (published in Boston, in 1952, by Little, Brown and Co.; and in London, in 1953, by MacGibbon & Kee) I described Le Catalan and gave recipes of three of its specialties. There have been certain minor changes in the restaurant since then. Now it is open for dinner only: excellent Spanish dancing is performed and authentic Flamenco music played while you leisurely enjoy certain new *spécialités de la maison*, such as the Paella à la Valencienne and Rognons Pamplona* (for which I give the recipe here). You are advised to book your table, for Le Catalan is, and will continue to be, very popular.

ROGNONS PAMPLONA
(LAMB KIDNEYS PAMPLONA)

Serves 4

1½ *cups Créole Rice**
½ *cup mushrooms, sliced*
Large walnut-size piece of
butter
8 *lamb kidneys*
1 *tablespoon olive oil*
1 *onion, chopped*
2 *cloves garlic, chopped*

1 *wineglass sherry*
3 *tomatoes, peeled, seeded,*
and chopped
½ *cup cooked peas*
Salt, pepper
Chopped parsley
2 *sweet red peppers*
(*canned*)

Start preparing the rice. Sauté the mushrooms gently, for about 5 minutes, in a little butter, in a large, deep frying pan. Remove and keep hot.

Cut the kidneys in half, chop them coarsely, and sauté them rapidly, in the very hot oil, for no more than 2 minutes. Add the chopped onion and allow to color, then the garlic and the butter. Stir gently and then pour in the sherry. Allow the sauce to reduce a little before adding the tomatoes. Cook for another 1 or 2 minutes then add the cooked peas and the mushrooms. Mix carefully together with a wooden spoon. Salt and pepper and remove at once.

Make a hollowed mold of the cooked rice in the middle of a serving dish. Pour the contents of the frying pan over the rice, sprinkle with the parsley, and decorate with the pre-heated red peppers, cut in julienne strips. Serve very hot.

PHARAMOND
24, Rue de la Grande Truanderie
Paris, 1er. Tel. Gutemberg 06–72
No closing day

SOUPE NORMANDE
(NORMANDY SOUP)

Serves 4

1 *pound potatoes, thinly sliced*	*Salt, pepper*
½ *pound carrots, finely*	*Toast*
chopped	*Small handful finely chopped*
2 *large leeks, sliced*	*chervil*
2 *tablespoons butter*	2 *tablespoons fresh cream*
3 *pints warm water*	

Stew the potatoes, carrots, and leeks in the butter in a small covered casserole over a low flame for about 10 minutes, or until they start to soften. Remove to a larger pan, pour in the warm water, salt and pepper, cover, and simmer for 40 minutes.

Meanwhile make thin slices of toast and add them to the soup, along with the chervil, just before serving. At the last minute, stir ½ tablespoon fresh cream into each plate of soup.

CANARD AUX PECHES
(DUCK WITH PEACHES)

Serves 4

1 4-pound duck	Beurre manié (1 ounce butter
Salt, pepper	mixed with ½ tablespoon
4 large fresh (or canned)	flour)
peaches	Croutons
2 tablespoons cognac	

Salt and pepper the duck and roast it for about 40 minutes in a hot oven. Meanwhile, poach the fresh, halved peaches in slightly sugared water (or else heat, gently, halved canned peaches in the oven).

Remove the duck and drain off the fat from the pan. Pour in the cognac, then incorporate the beurre manié, piece by piece. Stir well and bring to a boil. Allow to reduce by one third, then remove, pass through a fine sieve. Rectify the seasoning.

Cut up the duck and arrange on hot croutons on a serving dish. Arrange neatly the hot, halved peaches around the duck. Pour over the sauce and serve at once.

CHEZ PIERRE
10, Rue Richelieu and 7, Rue Montpensier
Paris, 1er.   Tel. Richelieu 36–41
Closed Sundays and during August

RABLE DE LAPIN A LA MOUTARDE
(SADDLE OF RABBIT WITH MUSTARD SAUCE)

Serves 4

1 saddle of rabbit	¼ cup fresh mustard
3 tablespoons butter	2 tablespoons fresh cream

Brown the saddle of rabbit slightly in the butter in a stewpan. Remove and smear the mustard all over it. Replace in the pan and cook, covered, over a medium flame, for 1 hour. Remove the rabbit, and place it on a hot serving dish. Remove the pan from the fire, add the cream, and stir well. Pass through a fine sieve and pour the sauce over the rabbit. Serve with new potatoes.

CHEZ PAUL
15, Place Dauphine and 52, Quai des Orfèvres
Paris, 1er. Tel. Odéon 21–48
Closed Mondays and during August

CREME VALDEZE
(CREAM OF BACON AND TOMATO SOUP)

Serves 4

2 *tablespoons olive oil*	*Bouquet garni*
1 *full cup lean bacon, diced*	*Salt, pepper*
2 *onions, finely chopped*	*Pinch cayenne*
1 *clove garlic, crushed*	3 *cups consommé*
4 *large fresh tomatoes, peeled*	1 *cup fresh cream, boiled*
and seeded	1 *glass port wine, warmed*
½ *cup rice*	

Brown slightly in the oil the diced bacon, the chopped onions, the crushed garlic, and, finally, add the tomatoes. Meanwhile poach the rice by bringing it to a boil. Remove at once and strain. Add the rice to the pan with the bouquet garni. Season with salt and pepper and the cayenne.

Pour the consommé into the pan. Cover and cook in a moderate oven for half an hour, after which time remove, discard the bouquet garni, and make a purée of the contents in the electric blender. Return to the pan and reheat. Remove and then stir in the hot cream and the warmed port wine. Serve at once.

CHEZ QUINSON
5, Place Félix-Faure
Paris, 15ème. Tel. Lecourbe 48–54
Closed Mondays and during August

IRISH STEW A LA PROVENCALE

Serves 6

2½ pounds boned shoulder of mutton or lamb
½ cup onions, chopped
2 cloves garlic, chopped
3 carrots, sliced
2 turnips, sliced
4 or 5 green cabbage leaves, cut in strips; or 3 or 4 leeks, sliced
7 tablespoons butter
Bouquet garni
Salt, pepper
2 pounds small potatoes (1 pound sliced; 1 pound whole)
24 baby onions
½ pound mushrooms, sliced
Worcestershire sauce
Parsley

Cut the mutton, or lamb, into cubes and soak in cold water. Remove, place in a stewpan, cover with water, and boil for 5 minutes. Strain and cool the pieces of meat under the tap. Replace in the rinsed pan.

Cook gently the chopped onions, the garlic, carrots, turnips, and the (previously blanched) cabbage leaves, or the leeks, in 3 tablespoons butter, along with the bouquet garni, in a small, well-covered casserole, until they start to soften. Add the vegetables to the mutton in the stewpan, salt and pepper and pour in sufficient warm water to cover, and cook over a low flame for three quarters of an hour, after which time add the sliced potatoes and leave to cook, covered, for another half an hour.

Remove the meat and place in another preheated pan. Take out the bouquet garni and pass the vegetables and the liquid through a sieve to make a purée, or better still, make a very fine purée in the electric blender. Add to the meat and reheat very slowly.

Meanwhile, boil the remaining whole potatoes, and cook the baby onions and the mushrooms gently, in 4 tablespoons butter, in a small covered pan (the onions will require to be cooked for double the length of time of the mushrooms). Add the onions and mushrooms to the stew, rectify the seasoning, and pour in the Worcestershire sauce (one or more tablespoons, according to taste). Stir well. Remove at once and place on a very hot serving dish with the whole potatoes, sprinkled with freshly chopped parsley, arranged around.

CHEZ OLIVIER
21, Rue Méderic
Paris, 17ème. Tel. Carnot 86–67
Closed Sundays and Mondays and from mid-July until mid-September

HOMARD GRILLE A LA DIABLE
(BLAZED GRILLED LOBSTER)

Serves 2

1 *lobster, of about 1½ pounds*	2 *tablespoons seasoned butter*
2 *tablespoons olive oil*	2 *tablespoons armagnac, or*
2 *tablespoons fresh cream*	*cognac*

Split the lobster in half lengthwise. You can first plunge it into boiling, salted water for 3 minutes. This will kill it instantly and make the flesh firmer.

Detach the claws. Pour the oil into a frying pan. When very hot, place in it the claws and the two halves of lobster, the cut side facing downwards. Press them down on to the pan for 3 or 5 minutes, then remove. Leave the claws in the pan for another 10 minutes.

Place the claws and the two halves of lobster in a shallow Pyrex dish with the cut side facing upwards. Spread a tablespoon of cream and a tablespoon of seasoned butter on each half of the lobster and grill for 12 minutes, basting frequently.

Remove the lobster and place on a very hot serving dish along with the claws broken. Pour over the warmed armagnac, or cognac, and blaze. Serve at once.

CHEZ MAITRE PAUL
12, Rue Monsieur-le-Prince
Paris, 6ème.   Tel. Odeon 74-59
Closed during August

LA POTEE
(COUNTRY STEW)

Serves 8 to 10

2½ pounds shoulder of cured salted pork
¾ pound breast of cured salted pork
4 quarts of water
Bouquet garni
5 cloves garlic
1 pound medium-sized carrots, halved
½ pound onions

1 pound small turnips, halved
¾ pound leeks, halved
2 pounds medium-sized potatoes, halved
1 large white cabbage, quartered
Pepper (no salt)
¾ pound cooking pork sausage
Croutons

Soak the shoulder and the breast of pork in water, for about 2 hours. Remove and rinse well. Place in an earthenware pot. Pour in the water. Bring to a boil and skim thoroughly. Lower the heat and add the bouquet garni and the garlic along with the carrots. A quarter of an hour later, add the onions; a quarter of an hour later, the turnips and the leeks; and, a quarter of an hour later, the cabbage (which should have been previously blanched for 5 minutes). Add the pepper. Simmer, covered, for one and a quarter hours, then add the potatoes and the pork sausage, pricked, to prevent it from bursting. Cook, covered, for another half an hour.

Strain the vegetables and arrange them neatly around a large, hot serving dish. In the middle, place the shoulder of pork cut in slices. On one side arrange the sliced pork sausage, on the other the breast of pork. The potatoes should be placed either end of the serving dish.

To serve the soup, strain the liquid through a sieve and pour into a tureen containing croutons.

ROTI DE VEAU THERMIDOR
(ROAST VEAL THERMIDOR)

Serves 8 to 10

¼ cup butter	2 pounds tomatoes, peeled,
3 pounds shoulder of veal	seeded, and chopped
Salt, pepper	2 cups fresh cream
½ cup dry white wine	

Heat the butter in a cocotte, or a stewpan, that will go into the oven. Brown the meat in the butter, on all sides. Salt and pepper, lower the heat and cook gently, covered, for about three quarters of an hour. Then add the white wine and an equal quantity of warm water. Add the tomatoes and cook, covered, for another three quarters of an hour, or until the veal is done.

Remove the meat from the stewpan and keep hot on a serving dish. Add the cream to the juice in the pan and cook gently, stirring with a wooden spoon, until the sauce thickens. Slice the veal and pour the sauce over the meat. Serve at once with new potatoes or Créole Rice.*

The cream will not turn during the cooking process so long as it is fresh and no flour has been added to the pan.

CHEZ GEORGES
34, Rue Mazarine
Paris, 6ème. Tel. Danton 69–49
Closed Mondays and during August

JAMBON FLORENTINE AU GRATIN
(HAM AND SPINACH AU GRATIN)

Serves 4

*Epinards à la crème**   ½ cup mixed, grated Parmesan
Butter   and Gruyère cheese
8 slices cooked ham   Madeira
1 cup Béchamel Sauce**

Prepare the:

EPINARDS A LA CREME (CREAMED SPINACH)

1½ pounds spinach   Salt, pepper
1 tablespoon butter   2 tablespoons cream
1 teaspoon flour

Wash thoroughly and cook the spinach. Drain and squeeze
out all the water. Chop and pass through the vegetable mill,
or make a purée of the spinach in the blender.

Make a roux with the butter and the flour. Add the spinach
and a little salt and pepper, stir well until the mixture starts
to dry, then add the cream. Bring gently to the boil and
simmer for 5 minutes, stirring with a wooden spoon.

Butter a shallow Pyrex dish and place in it 4 slices of ham
over which spread the creamed spinach. Cover with the other
4 slices of ham and pour over it the Béchamel Sauce. Sprinkle
with the grated cheese and brown in the oven for quarter of
an hour or until a light golden crust is formed. Just before
serving sprinkle about a teaspoon of Madeira over each portion
of ham and spinach.

CROQUE MOUJIC RUSSE
(BEEF MARROW ON TOAST)

Serves 4

Beef marrow   *Salt, pepper*
4 slices of bread, about 3
*   inches square*

Ask your butcher to remove the marrow from 2 large beef
marrow bones. Slice and place 6 rounds of marrow on each
piece of bread. Salt and pepper, place in a shallow baking
dish and cook in a very hot oven. As soon as the marrow is
golden color and starts to turn crisp on top, remove and
serve very hot with ice-cold vodka.

LE RUBAN BLEU
29, Rue d'Argenteuil
Paris, 1er.   Tel. Opéra 67–17
Closed Sundays and during August

ROGNONS FLAMBES RUBAN BLEU
(BLAZED KIDNEYS RUBAN BLEU)

Serves 4

¾ pound mushrooms, diced   *3 tablespoons cognac*
1 pound veal kidneys   *1 teaspoon strong mustard*
⅓ cup butter   *1 teaspoon Worcestershire*
Salt   *   sauce*
Freshly ground pepper   *2 tablespoons fresh cream*

Wash the mushrooms thoroughly and dice them. Blanch them
for 2 minutes in a little acidulated water (with lemon juice).
Strain and reserve. Remove the fat and sinews from the kidneys and also cut up into dice.

Cook the mushrooms and the kidneys together, for 4 or 5
minutes, in the butter, over a slow flame, in a small, heavy
copper pan. Season with a little salt and 10 or 11 turns of the

pepper mill. Pour in the cognac and ignite and keep shaking the pan. Add the cold, fresh cream, the mustard, and the Worcestershire sauce. Lower the heat immediately and cook very gently for about 3 or 4 minutes, shaking the pan all the time so as to sauté the contents. Serve at once on very hot plates.

Once the cold cream has been added to the pan, the dish must not come to a boil, otherwise the sauce will turn. All it requires is that the cream, mustard, and Worcestershire sauce become hot enough to bind the sauce.

COTES DE MOUTON CHAMPVALLON
(MUTTON CHOPS CHAMPVALLON)

Serves 4

4 thick mutton shoulder chops	*½ pound potatoes, thinly*
½ cup butter	*sliced*
½ cup onions, thinly sliced	*Salt, pepper*
1 clove garlic, crushed	*Chopped parsley*
Bouquet garni	*Consommé or bouillon*
Dry white wine	

Brown the chops on both sides, in a frying pan, in most of the butter. Remove the chops at once and keep warm in a Pyrex oven dish. Soften the onions in a walnut-sized piece of butter. Do not let them color. Spread the onions over the chops, add the garlic and the bouquet garni. Rinse the pan in which the chops have been browned with equal quantities of white wine and consommé or bouillon and pour over sufficient of the liquid so as to just cover the chops in the oven dish. Cover and cook in a medium oven for 20 minutes.

Remove the dish from the oven and strain off the juice into a small pan. Cover the chops with the sliced potatoes, salt and pepper, and pour back some of the reheated juice. Cook in the oven, adding now and again some more of the juice, for another 15 minutes or until the meat and potatoes are cooked.

Remove the bouquet garni and sprinkle the meat and potatoes with chopped parsley and serve straight from the dish. Serve Haricots Verts (French Beans)* separately.

LA CHOPE DANTON
4, Carrefour de l'Odéon
Paris, 6ème. Tel. Danton 67–76
Closed Mondays and during August

ROGNONS A LA MOUTARDE
(KIDNEYS WITH MUSTARD CREAM SAUCE)

Serves 4

4 small veal kidneys	*1 tablespoon oil*
Salt, pepper	*Sauce Moutarde à la crème**
2 tablespoons butter	

Cut the fat from the kidneys and slice them in half lengthwise. Salt and pepper them and brown quickly, on all sides, in the butter and oil, in a frying pan. When they take color, remove from the pan (discard the juice) and roast them in a hot oven for 5 minutes.

Meanwhile, prepare the:

SAUCE MOUTARDE A LA CREME

½ cup sliced mushrooms	*4 tablespoons fresh cream*
½ cup butter	*Salt and Pepper*
1½ cups very dry white wine	*2 tablespoons French mustard*

Sauté the mushrooms in the butter, in a small pan, for 2 or 3 minutes. Add the wine and then the cream. Stir well with a wooden spoon. Salt and pepper slightly and simmer for a few minutes. Remove the pan from the fire and stir in the mustard. Pour the sauce over the kidneys and serve at once.

LE GRAND COMPTOIR
4, Rue Pierre Lescot
Paris, 1er. Tel. Gutemberg 56–30
Closed Sundays

STEAK AU BEURRE D'ECHALOTES AVEC GRATIN DAUPHINOIS

(STEAK WITH SHALLOT BUTTER AND BAKED POTATOES AU GRATIN)

Serves 4

2 *tablespoons butter*	*Beurre d'Echalotes**
1 *tablespoon oil*	*Gratin Dauphinois**
4 *thick fillet steaks*	

Sear the steaks quickly, on either side, in the hot butter and oil. Lower the heat slightly and cook until done as required.

Meanwhile prepare the:

BEURRE D'ECHALOTES

¼ *cup butter*   2 *shallots, chopped very finely*

Melt the butter in a small pan. Add the shallots and cook very gently until the butter turns nut brown. Remove at once and pour over the steaks.

Serve with:

GRATIN DAUPHINOIS

3 *pounds potatoes, sliced*	½ *cup milk, scalded*
Butter	¼ *cup fresh cream*
Salt, pepper	½ *cup grated Parmesan cheese*

Take 3 pounds of even-sized potatoes. Peel them, wipe them well, and cut in slices. Butter a shallow Pyrex dish and arrange the sliced potatoes neatly in it. Salt and pepper and add sufficient warm water to reach one third of the level of the potatoes. Cover the Pyrex dish and place it on top of a protective asbestos pad over the gas or electric ring and cook for about 20 minutes, by which time the water, or most of it, should have evaporated.

Meanwhile, beat together the milk, cream, and ¼ cup of the grated cheese and bring to a boil. Pour over the potatoes and sprinkle with the rest of the grated cheese. Dot with small pieces of butter and brown gently in the oven until the potatoes are well cooked.

COQUILLES SAINT-JACQUES GRAND COMPTOIR
(SCALLOPS GRAND COMPTOIR)

Serves 3

4 *pounds scallops in their*   Beurre d'Escargot*
  shells   Salt, pepper
½ *cup butter*

Beard and wash thoroughly the scallops and brown them very gently in the butter in a heavy (copper) frying pan for about quarter of an hour.

Meanwhile, prepare the:
BEURRE D'ESCARGOT (SNAIL BUTTER)

6 *tablespoons butter*   ½ *tablespoon parsley, finely*
½ *clove garlic, crushed*   *chopped*
1 *tablespoon shallots, finely*   Salt, pepper
  chopped

Soften the butter and mix all the ingredients together into a smooth paste. As soon as the scallops are golden brown, remove from the pan and place on a hot serving dish. Liquefy and heat the beurre d'escargot and pour over the scallops and serve very hot.

The Back-Room Cooks
of the Latin Quarter

Most of my shopping is done in the Latin Quarter of Paris: we live on the Ile de la Cité, just by the Pont-Neuf, which leads you straight into it. Here you will find the very compact Marché de Buci and Marché de Saint-Germain-des-Près, two of the most animated, good-value-for-money markets in Paris, where I have been buying practically everything for our kitchen since more than twenty years ago. Consequently, I have got to know intimately all the merchants, shopkeepers and café proprietors in the quarter.

When I recently stepped into our local grocer's shop, in the Rue Dauphine, I instantly smelt something delicious being cooked in the kitchen, in the back room. Knowing the grocer and his wife to be natives of Auvergne, I asked if they were preparing a "plat du pays." "Yes," they said, with contented smiles, "and it's a Foie de Veau à l'Auvergnate."* I had heard of this dish before and was, naturally, curious to know how it was cooked. A day or two later, I obtained the detailed recipe for it, in addition to an intriguing vegetable dish, Chou Rouge aux Marrons.*

This inspired me to set out in search of other recipes from the back-room cooks of the Latin Quarter. I next went round the corner, to the Rue de Seine, to see my friends from whom I regularly buy their freshly made pasta (spaghetti, macaroni, tagliatelli, canelloni, ravioli, etc.). They are a very friendly couple from Antibes. *La patronne* loves cooking and enjoys talking about it on every occasion with her enchanting accent of the Midi. From her, I managed to obtain the "home" recipes for Tagliatelli à l'Antiboise* and the Tomates du Midi.*

One Sunday, when we were expecting friends in for lunch, I went to the Marché Saint-Germain to buy some turbot for my Filet de Turbot à l'Indienne dish.* But Louise, the buxom, good-humored fish vendor from Marseilles, had no turbot that day and I saw nothing on her usually very well stocked stall that could replace the dish I had intended to serve. "Take a look at those mackerel," she said. "They're superb and so fresh. They're line-caught, not net-fished." When Louise saw me retreat from the idea of offering our guests mackerel, she then divulged her own and ever-so-easy way of preparing Maquereaux en Papillote.* We tried it out, with great success. Among other recipes that Louise has since given me are her Oeufs Farcis au Thon.*

François, our butcher, wasn't quite so co-operative, at first, when I asked him to give me a few original ideas for preparing different cuts of meat. "The fact is," he said, "I get tired at looking at all this meat that I have to cut up and sell day in day out. Fortunately, my wife realizes this and she has recently been experimenting in our little back-room kitchen in dishes other than meat. A day or two ago she cooked an excellent Gibelotte de Lapin.* I'll ask her to give you the details; also for the Escalopes de Lapin."*

Nothing daunted, I next asked the proprietress of one of my favorite cafés—Le Lutetia, on the Quai de Bourbon—where light luncheons are served, what she could contribute by way of recipes for simple desserts. Her answer was to explain how easy it is to prepare Bananes Flambées* and the amusing Martinique Egg dish.*

And that is the way it goes in France today, world center of gastronomy. If you express a genuine interest in cooking, whether it be in conversation with the jovial Louise from Marseilles, who tells you how to cook Maquereaux en Papillote or Alexandre Dumaine, from Saulieu, the Chef No. 1 of

France, who reveals the secret of his magnificent Poularde au Vapeur de Pot-au-Feu, you can collect a mine of exciting and entertaining gastronomic information with which you can experiment in your own kitchen.

Hors d'Oeuvre:
    Oeufs Farcis au Thon (serves 2).

Fish:
    Maquereaux en Papillote (serves 4).

Entrées:
    Tagliatelli à l'Antiboise (serves 4).
    Tomates du Midi (serves 4).

Vegetable Dishes:
    Chou Rouge aux Marrons (serves 4).

Meat:
    Foie de Veau à l'Auvergnate (serves 6).

Rabbit:
    Gibelotte de Lapin (serves 4).
    Escalopes de Lapin (serves 2).

Desserts:
    Martinique Egg (serves 1).
    Bananes Flambées au Rhum (serves 4).

OEUFS FARCIS AU THON
(EGGS STUFFED WITH TUNA FISH)

Serves 2

4 hard-boiled eggs   *1 tablespoon butter*
2 ounces tuna fish in oil   *Salt, pepper*

Hardboil 4 eggs. Cool, peel, and cut them lengthways into two halves. Remove the yolks, pass them through a sieve together with the drained tuna fish and the butter. Place in a bowl.

Stir the mixture well with a spoon. Slice off a small piece from the whites of the eggs so that they can sit securely. Correct the seasoning. Place the mixture in a pastry bag, or cone, fitted with a decorator's tube, and fill each half egg in the shape of a mound.

To decorate, place a small round of tomato or green pepper on top of the eggs; or both, in alternative colors.

If desired, the eggs may be covered with gelatin. Leave to cool and arrange them neatly on a napkin.

MAQUEREAUX EN PAPILLOTE
(MACKEREL COOKED IN GREASEPROOF PAPER)

Serves 4

4 *medium-sized, very fresh mackerel*	*Salt, pepper*
Greaseproof paper	*French (tarragon) mustard*
Butcher's string	*Freshly chopped parsley*
2 *teaspoons butter*	1 *lemon, quartered*

Empty and clean the fish, and dry them. For each fish, cut a piece of greaseproof paper large enough so as to just enfold it and which can be tied securely either end (like a Christmas cracker).

Smear ½ teaspoon of butter and a little French (tarragon) mustard along the middle of each piece of paper. Salt and pepper the fish on both sides, place in the paper, enfold, and tie either end.

Place the four fish on a baking tray in a medium oven (or under the grill) and leave until the paper starts to get dark brown on top (about 15 to 20 minutes).

Remove the fish and place directly on to hot plates. Have a pair of kitchen scissors ready on the dining-room table with which your guests can cut away the ends of the papillotes. As you unroll the mackerel, most of its skin will come away. *This is a sign that it is properly cooked.* Serve with freshly chopped parsley and lemon quarters.

TAGLIATELLI A L'ANTIBOISE

(RIBBON NOODLES WITH HAM AND MUSHROOMS AU GRATIN)

Serves 4

Sauce Mornay*	*4 slices cooked ham, cut in*
1 egg yolk	*strips*
3 tablespoons grated	*½ cup mushrooms, sliced*
Parmesan cheese	*Bread crumbs*
3 tablespoons grated Gruyère	*2 tablespoons butter*
cheese	*Salt, pepper*
1 pound tagliatelli	

SAUCE MORNAY

This is a simplified version of Sauce Mornay. All it requires, for this dish, is to make rather a thick Sauce Béchamel.* Five or 6 minutes before removing the pan from the fire, incorporate the egg and 2 tablespoons each of grated Parmesan and Gruyère cheese into the sauce.

This dish looks and tastes better if the green tagliatelli (made with spinach) is used. Whether it be the green or the white tagliatelli, the important thing is that if just freshly made, the tagliatelli requires two minutes cooking only. If you are using packed tagliatelli, then it will need about 12 minutes' separate cooking in boiling salted water.

Divide the tagliatelli into four portions and the strips of ham into two portions. Sauté the mushrooms gently in the butter for 5 minutes.

Place a layer of the tagliatelli in the bottom of a hot buttered Pyrex dish and, on top, spread a portion of ham. Next, arrange a second layer of tagliatelli, and then the mushrooms. Then a third layer of tagliatelli, followed by the second portion of ham. Finish with the fourth layer of tagliatelli. Pour over the Sauce Mornay, sprinkle with the remaining tablespoons of grated Parmesan and Gruyère cheese, and then with the bread crumbs. Dot with tiny pieces of butter, place in the oven until nicely browned on top. Serve at once.

TOMATES DU MIDI
(PROVENCAL TOMATOES)

Serves 4

4 large, fresh, firm tomatoes
1 shallot, finely chopped
Butter
½ cup sausage meat
2 tablespoons cooked rice
   (whatever is left over from
   the Riz Créole*)

1 clove garlic, finely chopped
Freshly chopped parlsey and
   chervil
Salt, pepper
Olive oil
Bread crumbs

Slice off the top, the lid, of the tomatoes. Drain them of their water and seeds. Be careful not to bruise or break the skins. Leave inside just the pulp of the tomatoes.

Soften the finely chopped shallot in a little butter. Make a mixture of the sausage meat, the shallot, the rice, the garlic and herbs. Salt and pepper. Stuff the tomatoes. Pour a little olive oil into a preheated Pyrex dish. Sprinkle the tomatoes with bread crumbs, place a small piece of butter on top of each, arrange in the Pyrex dish and cook in a medium oven for 20 minutes, or until the tomatoes start to soften. Serve at once.

CHOU ROUGE AUX MARRONS
(RED CABBAGE WITH CHESTNUTS)

Serves 4

2 pounds chestnuts
1 medium-sized red cabbage,
   quartered
¾ cup bacon, diced

¼ cup butter
2 eating apples, peeled, and
   quartered

Remove the brown, outer skin of the chestnuts. Plunge them into boiling water, cover and leave for 5 minutes. Drain them in cold water and then remove the inner skin. Cook the well-skinned chestnuts in water for about one hour or until they start to get tender.

Meanwhile, quarter the cabbage. Remove the core and outer leaves and boil until it starts to soften.

Sauté the diced bacon, in the butter, in the bottom of stewpan and then add the strained chestnuts. When all is nicely browned, cover with the strained cabbage leaves and place the two quartered apples on top. Add a little of the water in which the cabbage has cooked. Cover and simmer for 10 minutes.

This is a dish that can be reheated. Retain some of the water in which the cabbage has cooked in the event of the contents of the pan requiring more liquid.

GIBELOTTE DE LAPIN
(FRICASSEE OF RABBIT)

Serves 4

1 *rabbit for 4 persons*	*Salt, pepper*
¼ *cup dripping*	24 *baby onions*
Flour	1 *cup bacon, diced*
2 *cloves garlic, finely chopped*	¼ *cup butter*
Red wine and water in equal quantities	1 *pound small new potatoes*
	Chopped parsley

Cut up the rabbit and brown it in the dripping in a stewpan. Dust with flour, add the garlic and sufficient, equal quantities of red wine and water to cover the meat. Season with salt and pepper. Stir well. Bring to the boil, cover, lower the heat and cook gently for half an hour, then add the onions and the diced bacon (which have been previously browned in the butter).

Meanwhile, boil the potatoes. By the time the fricassee has cooked for another 20 minutes, after the onions and bacon have been added, the potatoes themselves should be ready to add to the pan. Cook all together very gently for another 10 minutes or so.

Pour the fricassee into a preheated serving dish, sprinkle with finely chopped fresh parsley, and bring straight to the table.

FOIE DE VEAU A L'AUVERGNATE
(CALF'S LIVER A L'AUVERGNATE)

Serves 6

2 pounds calf's liver
Larding pork
12 small onions

½ cup butter
2 tablespoons fresh cream
Salt, pepper

Wrap the piece of liver in larding pork and brown on all sides, along with the onions, in the butter, in a copper casserole. Salt and pepper, cover securely, and cook gently for three quarters of an hour. *From time to time, raise carefully the lid of the casserole and tilt it so that the water formed by the steam drips back into the liquid, making a natural sauce.*

When the liver is cooked, remove the larding pork and place on a hot serving dish along with the onions. Remove the casserole from the fire, stir in the cream and pour the sauce over the liver. Serve very hot with braised Belgian endives and steamed potatoes.

ESCALOPES DE LAPIN
(ESCALOPES OF RABBIT)

Serves 2

2 slices from the back of a rabbit
Salt, pepper
1 egg, beaten
Bread crumbs

Butter
2 small thin slices of ham
2 slices of fresh tomatoes
2 small very thin slices of Gruyère cheese

Cut two good-sized slices from the back of a rabbit. Bone them and beat carefully each piece into escalopes. Season and roll in the beaten egg and then in the bread crumbs. Sauté in butter for 5 or 6 minutes.

Place a slice of ham on top of each escalope, next a slice of tomato and, finally, the slice of cheese. Place in a medium oven so as to make the cheese start to melt. Remove and serve hot with a little of the nut-brown butter from the pan poured over the escalopes.

MARTINIQUE EGG

Serves 1

1 *individual portion coffee ice cream*
1 *slice pineapple (fresh or canned)*
½ *peach (fresh or canned)*
Crème Chantilly (whipped cream)
Rum

This is a decorative and very easily prepared dessert. It involves no cooking!

Place the coffee ice cream on top of the pineapple. Cap it with the halved peach and arrange the cream over and around the pineapple and almost to the top of the peach, so that it looks like a fried egg. Pour over a little good-quality rum and serve chilled.

BANANES FLAMBEES AU RHUM
(BANANAS BLAZED WITH RUM)

Serves 4

8 *bananas*
¼ *cup butter*
Brown sugar
Lemon juice
½ *cup rum*

Peel and split lengthwise eight not too ripe bananas. Melt the butter in a shallow baking or Pyrex dish, and in it arrange the halved bananas, round side uppermost. Sprinkle lightly with brown sugar and place in a hot oven. After 10 minutes, squeeze a few drops of lemon juice over the bananas. Baste and replace in the oven for another 3 or 4 minutes.

Meanwhile, warm the rum. Baste the bananas carefully once more before removing from the oven. Bring the dish straight to the table, pour over the rum, and blaze.

French Index

poireaux, 40
velouté de grouse Saint-
Hubert, 29
Pot-au-feu à la langue de veau,
62
Pot-au-feu Alexandre, 66
Potée, 134
Poularde Marie-Louise, 107
Poule au pot, 58
Poulet
au blanc, 113
de ferme étuvé à la digoi-
naise, 32
flambé, 57
poularde Marie-Louise, 107
poule au pot, 58
sauté à l'estragon, 119
sauté paysanne, 89
Purée de pommes de terre, 30,
101

Rable de lapin à la moutarde,
130
Ratatouille, 115
Risi-bisi, 125
Riz à l'amande, 81
Riz créole, 73
Rognonnade de veau printani-
ère, 63
Rognons d'agneau Pamplona,
128
Rognons de veau
à la moutarde, 139
flambés Ruban Bleu, 137
sautés, 101
Turbigo, 126
Rôti de veau thermidor, 135

Saint-Pierre, filets de, 54
Salade
chinoise, 79
des orfèvres, 80

Fi-fi, 80
Nicoise, 122
Sauce
Bagnarotte, 43
béchamel, 100
blanche, 76
Dominique, 123
hollandaise, 54
mayonnaise, 51
Mornay, 148
moutarde à la crème, 139
piquante, 62
tomate, 46
vinaigrette, 80
Sauté de veau Marengo, 64
Soupe
à la tomate, 41
à l'oignon gratinée, 40
normande, 129
V. Potages et soupes
Steak
au beurre d'échalotes, 140
au poivre Albert, 120
moyen âge, 69
tartare, 67

Tagliatelli à l'Antiboise, 148
Terrine de foies de volaille
truffée, 110
Tomates
du Midi, 149
Lucien, 95
Tomate, sauce, 46
Turbot, filets de, à l'indienne,
49

Veau
blanquette de, 117
côtes de, aux cepes, 93
épaule de, aux oignons, 61
foie de, à l'Auvergnate, 151
foie de, aux raisins secs, 65

English Index